John Fred Stein

German Exercises

Material to Translate into German

John Fred Stein

German Exercises
Material to Translate into German

ISBN/EAN: 9783337189518

Printed in Europe, USA, Canada, Australia, Japan

Cover: Foto ©Thomas Meinert / pixelio.de

More available books at **www.hansebooks.com**

GERMAN EXERCISES.

MATERIAL TO TRANSLATE INTO

GERMAN.

By

J. FRED. STEIN,

INSTRUCTOR OF GERMAN IN THE BOSTON HIGH SCHOOLS.

BOSTON:

GINN & COMPANY

1888.

PREFACE.

DURING my experience of many years in teaching German I have constantly felt the want of material suitably graded, for translating into German. I have searched and inquired everywhere, but have not succeeded in finding what I was in need of; it is true, there are books prepared for that purpose, but none of them seemed to me just the thing needed. The contents of these books are either too classical and therefore too uninteresting, or, again, consist mostly of anecdotes which are found more or less literally in any German reader.

As I have always been of the opinion that this kind of work should be begun early, I was obliged to prepare something adapted to the progressive needs of my classes ; but this generally consumed a great deal of valuable time, since this material had to be copied. In this way I have, in the course of a number of years, accumulated sufficient material for a three or four years' course.

Having been urged repeatedly by teachers of high standing, who knew of my work, to collect and arrange my exercises for publication, I have at length decided to put together these pieces just as I have given them to my classes, when they were ready to begin translating connected matter into German.

It remains for me to acknowledge, with thanks, the assistance I have received from the gentlemen named below, in compiling this book : MR. J. TETLOW, Head Master of the Girls' High and Latin Schools, has given me the most invaluable suggestions after reading a part of my manuscript; as also MR. J. NORRIS, Head Master of Charlestown High School, and MR. S. THURBER, Master in the Girls' High School, have made necessary corrections in my English work.

I also extend my thanks to MR. C. H. HEINTZEMANN, who, through his care and personal attention to the typography, has given a pleasing appearance to this little book.

INTRODUCTION.

As every one knows who has studied German, the construction is of the greatest importance, and the rules on this subject must be given in the briefest and clearest form. I have therefore devoted a few pages at the outset to a preliminary statement of such facts and principles as are indispensable to beginners. Other necessary hints will be given in connection with the notes and vocabularies.

It further seemed desirable to me that in a book of this kind the notes should not be given in the form of references to any particular grammar, but should be complete in themselves, so as to be used in connection with any text-book. The first exercises may be begun as soon as the rudiments of any grammar in general use have been studied, and the grammar and this book may go hand in hand for some time.

I have found in my experience that pupils of good ability will begin the exercises contained in this little book and see their way quite clear when they have mastered the regular forms of the declensions of nouns and adjectives, the cases used after a few common prepositions, the conjugation of the auxiliary verbs and the formation of the tenses of regular verbs. The aim of this book is, in fact, to make the pupil practically acquainted with the parts of speech and the common construction of the language, after a general acquaintance with the regular forms has been gained.

5

ARRANGEMENT OF WORDS IN PRINCIPAL DECLARATORY SENTENCES.

Subject.	Personal Verb.	Adverb of time.	Objects. Dative.	Objects. Accusative.	Negations.	All Adverbs or adverbial expressions not of time.	Past Participle or Infinitive or Predicate Adj.
1. Der Knabe / The boy	hat / has			sein Buch / his book		in der Schule / in school	
2. Der Knabe / The boy	hat / has	heute / to-day		sein Buch / his book		in der Schule / in school	gehabt. / had.
3. Der Knabe / The boy	hat / has	gestern / yesterday		sein Buch / his book		in der Schule / in school	haben. / have.
4. Der Knabe / The boy	wird / will	morgen / to-morrow		sein Buch / his book		in der Schule / in school	gehabt haben. / have had.
5. Dieser Knabe / This boy	würde / would	gestern / yesterday		sein Buch / his book		in der Schule / in school	gehabt. / had.
6. Dieser Knabe / This boy	hat / has	gestern / yesterday		sein Buch / his book	nicht / not	in der Schule / in school	gehabt. / had.
7. Der Mensch / Man	ist / is						sterblich. / mortal.
8. Der Vater / The father	hat / has	gestern / yesterday		einen Hut / a hat		für seinen Sohn in einem Hutladen in Boston / for his son in a hat-store in Boston	gelauft. / bought.
9. Der Vater / The father	hat / has	gestern / yesterday	seinem Sohn / his son	einen Hut / a hat		in einem Hutladen in Boston / in a hat-store in Boston	gelauft. / bought.

GERMAN EXERCISES.

——•◦•——

Inversion of Construction (Verb before the Subject).

I. In the following instances as in English : —

(*a*) In interrogative sentences :

1. Wann hat der Knabe sein Buch nicht in der Schule gehabt?
When has the boy, etc.

2. Wo hat der Knabe gestern sein Buch nicht gehabt?
Where has the boy, etc.

3. Hat der Mann sein Geld gefunden?
Has the man his money found?

4. Haben Sie das neue Haus gekauft?
Have you the new house bought?

(*b*) In imperative sentences :

5. Schreiben Sie einen Brief an Ihren Onkel!
Write (you) a letter to your uncle!

(*c*) In exclamatory sentences :

6. Sollte das Kind gefallen sein!
Should the child fallen be = have fallen!

(*d*) In conditional sentences when the conjunction "if" (wenn) is omitted, which may be done at any time in German :

7. Hätte der Knabe heute sein Buch nicht in der Schule gehabt.
Had the boy to-day his book not in school had.

8. Wäre der Knabe zwei Jahre älter.
Were the boy two years older.

II. In the following case the German order differs
from the English : —

In a simple sentence, any other word than the subject may,
and often does, come first; this places the verb before the
subject (inversion); this usage generally occurs with adverbs
of time:

    1. Geſtern hat der Knabe ſein Buch nicht in der Schule
       gehabt.
       Yesterday the boy has, etc.

    2. Einen Hut hat der Vater geſtern ſeinem Sohn in einem
       Laden in Boſton gekauft.
       A hat the father has yesterday, etc.

(The foregoing sentences should be made fully clear by the teacher.)

Remarks on some Subordinate Conjunctions.

(a) *When ?* = wann? asking for time in direct or indirect
    questions.

(b) *If* = wenn, in conditional clauses, after imperf. or plu-
    perf. tenses, subjunctive mode.

(c) *When* = wenn, followed by the present, perfect, or future
    tense.

(d) *When, as* = als, speaking of time, followed by the imperf.
    or pluperf. tense, when a single fact is spoken of;
    otherwise, wenn.

(e) *As, since* = da, expressing cause.

(f) *Since* = ſeit, or ſeitdem, expressing time only.

(g) *If, whether* = ob, in indirect questions; subjunctive
    mode after imperf. or pluperf. tense.

(h) *As if* = als ob, subj. mode after imperf. or pluperf. tense.

EXAMPLES ILLUSTRATING THE FOREGOING CONJUNCTIONS.

(a) When? = wann?

1. Wann können Sie kommen? — *Direct.*
   When can you come?
2. Wissen Sie, wann Sie kommen können? — *Indirect.*
   Do you know when you can come?

(b) If = wenn.

1. Wenn sie hier wäre.
   If she were here.
2. Wenn er sein Geld nicht verloren hätte.
   If he his money not lost had.

(c) When = wenn.

1. Wenn ich jetzt nach Hause komme.
   When I now come home.
2. Wenn ich meine Aufgabe geschrieben habe.
   When I my exercise written have.

(d) When, as = als.

1. Als mein Bruder nach Hause kam.
   When (as) my brother home came.
2. Als der Schüler seine Aufgabe gelernt hatte.
   When (as) the scholar his lesson learned had.

(e) As, since = da.

1. Da es heute regnet.
   As (since) it to-day rains.
2. Da der Knabe nicht fleißig ist.
   As (since) the boy not industrious is.

(f) Since = seit.

1. Seit (or seitdem) sie hier ist.
   Since (the time) she here is.

2. Seitdem er auf dem Lande ist.
Since (the time) he in the country is.

(g) If, whether = ob.

1. Er fragte mich, ob mein Freund krank wäre.
He asked me if (whether) my friend ill were.

2. Der Lehrer fragte ihn, ob er seine Aufgabe gelernt hätte.
The teacher asked him if (whether) he his lesson learned had.

(h) As if = als ob.

1. Es scheint, als ob es schneien würde.
It seems as if (as though) it snow would.

2. Er spricht, als ob er alles wüßte.
He speaks as if (though) he everything knew.

All other conjunctions have only one meaning.

Arrangement of Words in Subordinate Clauses.

The following three parts of speech require the personal verb at the end of their respective clauses:—

1. **Subordinate Conjunctions.**
2. **Relative Pronouns.**
3. **Interrogative Adverbs and Pronouns in not direct questions.**

(a) Principal simple sentence:

Der Vater hat gestern seinem Sohn einen Hut in einem Hutladen in Boston gekauft.

(b) Compound sentence with coordinate conjunction (no change of construction):

Der Vater ist gestern in Boston gewesen und hat seinem Sohn einen Hut in einem Hutladen gekauft.

The father has yesterday in Boston been, and has his son a hat in a hat-store bought.

I. Subordinate Conjunctions.

Compound sentence with subordinate clause : —

> Der Vater kaufte seinem Sohn einen Hut, als er gestern in Boston war.
>
> The father bought his son a hat, when he yesterday in Boston was.

It will be seen that, when the principal clause introduces the sentence, and the dependent clause takes the second place, the latter does not disturb the former; but if the principal clause takes the second place, the verb comes before the subject, as :

Als der Vater gestern in Boston war, kaufte er seinem Sohn einen Hut.

> *Examples:* 1. Es war neun Uhr, als mein Freund heute nach Boston kam.
>
> It was nine o'clock, when my friend to-day to Boston came.
>
> 2. Wenn ich jetzt nach Hause komme, werde ich meine Aufgabe schreiben.
>
> When I now home come, will I my lesson write.
>
> 3. Als mein Freund heute nach Boston kam, war es neun Uhr.
>
> 4. Ich werde meine Aufgabe schreiben, wenn ich jetzt nach Hause komme.

II. Relative Pronouns.

> Der Vater, welcher gestern in Boston war, hat seinem Sohn einen Hut gekauft.
>
> The father, who yesterday in Boston was, has his son a hat bought.

The relative clause, as will be seen, does not affect the order of the principal clause.

III. Interrogative Pronouns and Adverbs in not Direct Questions.

Direct Question: Wie heißt der Vater, welcher seinem Sohn einen Hut kaufte, als er gestern in Boston war?

What is the name of the father, who his son a hat bought, when he yesterday in Boston was?

Indirect Question: Wissen Sie, wie der Vater heißt, welcher seinem Sohn einen Hut kaufte, als er gestern in der Stadt Boston war?

Do you know what the father's name is, who his son a hat bought when he yesterday in the city of Boston was?

(This last sentence contains the three parts of speech.)

Several subordinate clauses may come together in one compound sentence ; but this makes no other change in the construction than as if there were only one there ; for example :

Als ich diesen Morgen in die Schule kam, sagte mir mein Nachbar, — daß wir heute keine Zeichenstunde haben würden, — weil der Zeichenlehrer, — welcher seit einiger Zeit nicht sehr wohl gewesen ist, — heute nicht in die Schule kommen könnte, — da er gestern Abend plötzlich sehr krank wurde.

When I came to school this morning, my neighbor told me — that we would have no drawing-lesson to-day — because the drawing-teacher, — who has not been very well for some time, — could not come to school to-day — as he became suddenly very ill last night.

EXCEPTION: When the auxiliary verb haben in a dependent clause would be required at the end, and is then preceded by two infinitives, or an infinitive and a past part., it stands before the two latter, as :

1. Der Knabe, welcher gestern nicht hat schreiben wollen ; not schreiben wollen hat.
   The boy who has not wished to write yesterday = who did not wish to write yesterday.

2. Nachdem ich ihn hatte rufen lassen ; not rufen lassen hatte.
   After I had him called. (Werden is in most cases used in the same way.)

As this work is not intended for a grammar, the foregoing must suffice so far as matters of construction are concerned; other peculiarities will be explained in the notes.

NOTE: What has been said on the construction must not be supposed to be always strictly observed. Change of meaning, euphony, and often the choice of a writer, cause departure from the rules above given. But it is safe to assert, that the student who observes these rules will in no instance make a serious mistake in construction. The usage of recognized good prose writers, and the conversation of cultivated society, can be the only safe and sure guide.

On Auxiliaries of Compound Past Tenses of Verbs.

Haben is used with:

1. All transitive verbs, as: Ich habe gemacht, gesehen, geschrieben, I have made, seen, written.

2. Impersonal verbs, as: Es hat gedonnert, geregnet, geblitzt, it has thundered, rained, lightened.

3. Reflective verbs, as: Es hat mich gereut, gefreut, I have regretted, it has pleased me.

4. All those intransitives which govern:

   (a) Genitive, as: Ich habe seiner gedacht, I have thought of him.

   (b) Dative, as: Ich habe ihm gedankt, I have thanked him.

   (c) Which express a state or condition, or a continuous activity, as:

   State or condition: Ich habe geschlafen, I have slept (been asleep).

   Continuous action: Ich habe gearbeitet, sie hat genäht, I have worked, she has sewed.

EXCEPTIONS: Sein is used with: Bleiben (to remain), sein (to be), gelingen (to succeed), geschehen (to happen), and a few more.

Sein is used with all intransitive verbs which indicate:

(a) A motion or change of place: Ich bin gegangen, gekommen, gefallen, I have gone, come, fallen.

(*b*) A change of condition: Er ist gestorben, es ist warm geworden, he has died, it has grown warm.

There is still another class of verbs that express motion, which take sometimes haben and sometimes sein. They take haben when used without limitation of place, as:

Er hat gesprungen, er hat geschwommen, er hat geeilt.
He has jumped,   he has swum,   he has hastened.

But when used with a limitation of place, they take sein, as:

1. Er ist auf den Stuhl gesprungen.
   He has jumped upon the chair.
2. Er ist über den Fluß geschwommen.
   He has swum over the river.
3. Er ist nach Hause — zu dem Doctor geeilt.
   He has hastened home, — to the doctor.

In order to accustom the pupil's ear to the German sound, some material is given here for conversation, and at the same time for construction:

1. Ich habe gestern einen Mann gesehen.
   I have seen a man yesterday.

Wer? who? — **wen?** whom? — **wann?** when?

Question: Wer hat gestern einen Mann gesehen?
Answer: Ich habe gestern einen Mann gesehen.
Qu.: Wen haben Sie gestern gesehen?
Ans.: Einen Mann habe ich, etc.
Qu.: Wann haben Sie einen Mann gesehen?
Ans.: Gestern habe ich, etc.

It should be remembered right at the outset, that the answer to a question should always form a complete sentence, and that it should begin with the word or expression which directly answers the interrogative word; if that is any other word but the subject, it will cause an inversion.

2. Ich habe gestern einen Mann in dem Garten gesehen.
I have seen a man in the garden yesterday.

Wo? where?

Qu.: Wo haben Sie gestern einen Mann gesehen?
Ans.: In dem Garten habe ich gestern, etc.

3. Ich habe gestern Nachmittag einen Mann in dem Obst=
garten meines Nachbars gesehen.
I have seen a man in the orchard of my neighbor (my
neighbor's orchard) yesterday afternoon.

Was für ein? what, what kind of a?—Wessen? whose?

Qu.: In was für einen Garten haben Sie, etc.?
Ans.: In einem Obstgarten habe ich, etc.

4. Ich habe letzten Donnerstag einen Mann mit einem Knaben
in dem Obstgarten meines Onkels gesehen.
I have seen a man with a boy in the orchard of my
uncle last Thursday.

Mit wem? with whom?

Qu.: Mit wem haben Sie letzten Donnerstag, etc.?
Ans.: Mit einem Knaben habe ich letzten Donnerstag, etc.

As many questions may be asked as the pupils can answer
with their stock of interrogative adverbs and pronouns.

5. Der Mann in dem Obstgarten meines Onkels heißt Herr
Schwarz, und sein Sohn heißt Karl.
The name of the man in orchard of my uncle is Mr.
Schwarz, and his son's name is Carl.

Ich heiße, my name is; du heißest, er, sie, es heißt.
Sie heißen, your name is.

Wie heißt der Mann? What is the man's name?
Wie heißt er, sie? What is his, her name?

Wie heißen Sie?   What is your name?

Wie heißt das?   What do you call that?

Qu.:   Wie heißt der Mann mit dem Knaben, etc.?

Ans.:   Herr Schwarz heißt der Mann, etc.

Qu.:   Wie heißt sein Sohn?

Ans.:   Karl heißt sein Sohn.

Welcher, welche, welches? which?

Qu.:   Welcher Mann heißt Herr Schwarz?

Ans.:   Der Mann in dem Obstgarten heißt Herr Schwarz.

So *ad infinitum* questions may be asked, all of which the pupils will be able to answer readily after a very short time.

6. Der Mann hatte einen Stock in der rechten Hand und einen großen, reifen Apfel in der linken.

 The man has a stick in his right hand, and a large ripe apple in his left hand.

Was? what?

Qu.: In welcher Hand hatte der Mann einen, etc.? Was hatte der Mann in der linken, was in der rechten Hand? Was für einen Apfel hatte der Mann, etc., etc.

7. Der Stock ist gewöhnlich von Holz gemacht.

 The stick is usually made of wood.

Von was? of what? — Usually, gewöhnlich. — Holz, n., wood.

Qu.:   Von was ist gewöhnlich ein Stock gemacht?

Ans.:   Von Holz ist ein Stock gewöhnlich, etc.

8. Der Apfel ist eine Frucht und wächst auf einem Apfelbaum.

 The apple is a fruit and grows on an apple-tree.

9. Einige Äpfel sind rund, andere sind lang; einige sind süß, andere sauer.

 Some apples are round, others are long; some are sweet, others sour.

Einige, some; andere, others.

Qu.: War dieſer Apfel rund oder lang; ſüß oder ſauer?

10. Der Vater hat dieſen Apfel unter einem Apfelbaum gefun=
    den; er hat ſeinem Sohn den Apfel gegeben und ſein
    Sohn hat den Apfel gegeſſen.

    The father has found this apple under an apple-tree ; he
    has given his son the apple and his son has eaten
    the apple.

Gefunden, found. — gegeben, given. — gegeſſen, eaten.

Qu.: Was hat ſein Sohn mit dem Apfel gethan (done) ?
Ans.: Sein Sohn hat den Apfel gegeſſen.

12. Sein Sohn ißt die Äpfel (pl.) gern.
    His son likes (to eat) apples.

Ich eſſe gern, I like to eat;   ich trinke gern, I like to drink.
Du iſſeſt gern, you like to eat; ich leſe gern, I like to read.
Er, ſie, es ißt gern, he, she, it   ich gehe gern, I like to go.
    likes to eat.

The adverb **gern** with a verb gives it the meaning of liking ;
comparative, **lieber** ; superlative, **am liebſten.**

Ich eſſe gern,	ich eſſe lieber,	ich eſſe am liebſten.
I like to eat,	I like better,	I like best.
Ich trinke gern,	ich trinke lieber,	ich trinke am liebſten.
Ich gehe gern,	ich gehe lieber,	ich gehe am liebſten, etc.

Form questions and answers from the following words :

Apfel, *m.*, pl. Äpfel. Birne, *f.*, pl. Birnen. Kirſche, *f.*, pl.
—en. Brot, *n.*, Kuchen, *m.*, Fleiſch, *n.*, Kaffee, *m.*, Thee, *m.*,
Waſſer, *n.*, Milch, *f.*, Schule, *f.*, Kirche, *f.*, Theater, *n.*, Concert, *n.*

Qu.: Eſſen Sie gern Äpfel ?
Ans.: Ich eſſe nicht gern Äpfel, or ich eſſe Äpfel nicht gern, or
    gern.

    Qu.: Ißt er lieber Birnen als (or ober) Kirſchen?

    Ans.: Er ißt lieber Kirſchen.

    Qu.: Was ißt ſie am liebſten: Brot, Kuchen ober Fleiſch?

    Ans.: Sie ißt am liebſten Kuchen, etc.

13. *Qu.:* Wer iſt unſer Onkel? (unſer — our.)

    Ans.: Unſer Onkel iſt ber Bruber unſeres Vaters ober unꞏ
ſerer Mutter.

14. *Qu.:* Wer iſt unſere Tante?

    Ans.: Unſere Tante iſt die Schweſter unſerer Mutter
ober unſeres Vaters.

Form similar questions and answers from following words:

Tante, *f.* Nichte, *f.* (niece). Neffe, *m.* (nephew). Vetter,
m. (male cousin). Großmutter, *f.* Großvater, *m.*

These questions may be asked and at first answered with the
book open, and then without any assistance.

The original text, on which the exercises set for translation
into German are based, will be given for some time to come, in
order to lead the pupil on until more assurance is felt; it will,
however, be omitted when it may reasonably be expected that
the pupil can work more independently.

The German material must be thoroughly explained to the
pupil, who should be well acquainted with the German and
the English; if there is time enough, the German anecdote
should be committed to memory before the translation of the
corresponding English is begun.

The teacher should at the beginning write the translation
upon the board, having one of the class dictate a sentence. In
this way the class may take part in correcting the work, and
each pupil will see the mistakes made and listen to explanation
given in regard to them; after a time as many of the class as
find room at the board may write at the same time, and the
whole translation may be put on the board in a very short time;
and they all must be ready to follow the corrections.

PART FIRST.

1. Nicht zu Hause.[1]

Leſſing kam[2] eines Abends[3] nach Hauſe und klopfte[4] an ſeine Thür. Der Diener ſah[5] aus dem Fenſter, erkannte[6] aber ſeinen Herrn im Dunkeln[7] nicht und rief[8]: „Der Profeſſor iſt nicht zu Hauſe." „Schadet nichts[9]," antwortete Leſſing, „ich werde ein andermal[10] wieder kommen," und ging[11] ruhig[12] fort.[13]

[1] not at home. [2] to come, kommen, kam, ich bin gekommen. [3] one evening; indefinite time, genitive; definite, accusative. [4] to knock. [5] to see, to look, ſehen, ſah, geſehen. [6] to recognize, erkennen, erkannte, erkannt. [7] in the dark. [8] to call, to cry, rufen, rief, gerufen. [9] no matter. [10] another time. [11] to go, gehen, ging, ich bin gegangen. [12] quietly. [13] away.

When the auxiliary for the perfect tense is not given, the verb uses haben.

MATERIAL FORMED FROM THE ORIGINAL TEXT.

1a. — Not at Home.

Lessing knocked at his door when[1] he came home one evening. His servant, who[2] was in the house, looked out of the window; but he did not recognize him, as[3] it was dark, and said: "The professor is not yet[4] at home." Lessing, who had his thoughts[5] elsewhere,[6] replied: "No matter, I will call again some other time," and went away.

[1] when, als, subord. conj. [2] who, welcher, welche, welches, or der, die, das. [3] as, da, sub. conj. [4] not yet, noch nicht. [5] thought, Gedanke, m., pl. -en. [6] elsewhere, ſonſtwo.

19

1b.

When Lessing came home one evening it was quite[1] late,[2] and he found[3] his door locked.[4] He rang[5] the bell,[5] so that[6] they[7] should[8] hear him in the house. His servant, who had been asleep,[9] heard him and looked out of a window; but as (there) was no light before the house, it was so dark that he could[10] not recognize him. He said then to his master: "The professor is not yet at home." Lessing, having[11] his thoughts elsewhere, did not notice[12] the mistake[13] his servant had made,[14] and went away.

[1] quite, ziemlich. [2] late, ſpät. [3] to find, finden, fand, gefunden. [4] to lock, ſchließen, ſchloß, geſchloſſen. [5] to ring the bell, klingeln (reg.). [6] so that, ſo daß, or daß (sub. conj.). [7] they, man (is followed by third person sing. only). [8] shall, ſollen, ſollte, geſollt. [9] to be asleep, to sleep: ſchlafen, du ſchläfſt, er ſchläft, ſchlief, geſchlafen (if the second and third persons of sing., present tense, indic. mode, of an irregular verb is not given, the root-vowel does not change). [10] can: können, ich kann, du kannſt, er kann, wir können, etc., konnte, gekonnt. [11] having (the English pres. part. in the progressive form is in German rendered in various ways, which will be spoken of as they occur; here it is best to translate it by the relative pronoun, as: Lessing, who had, etc. [12] did notice, noticed, bemerken (reg.). [13] Irrtum (m.). [14] to make, machen (reg.). "his servant had made," a relative pronoun omitted in English must be translated in German.

---

2. Gutes Geſchäft.[1]

Zwei Reiſende[2] kauften[3] an einem warmen Tage im Sommer zuſammen[4] ein Pferd. „Wenn ich reite[5]," ſagte der Eine, „ſo gehſt du, und wenn du gehſt, ſo reite ich," und der Andere war mit dem Geſchäft zufrieden.[6]

[1] good bargain. [2] traveller. [3] to buy. [4] together. [5] to ride. [6] satisfied.

2a. — A Good Bargain.

Two men made a journey[1] one day in summer. It was a very hot day and, as they were very tired,[2] they bought a horse together. The question³ now⁴ was, who shall⁵ (is going to) ride on⁶ that horse? One then said to⁷ the other: "When I ride, you will walk, and when you walk, I will ride," and the other one was perfectly⁸ satisfied with the bargain.

¹ Reise (f.). ² müde. ³ Frage (f.). ⁴ nun. ⁵ shall, soll. ⁶ on, auf (dat. after verb of rest). ⁷ to, zu (dative). ⁸ vollkommen.

---

3. Früh aufstehen.¹

Ein Vater wünschte einmal, daß sein Sohn früh aufstehen sollte, und erzählte² ihm die Geschichte von einer Person, welche früh am Morgen eine Börse³ mit Gold gefunden⁴ habe.⁴ „Ja," sagte der Knabe, „aber die Person, welche das Gold verloren⁵ hat, ist doch⁶ noch⁷ früher aufgestanden."

¹ to rise early, early rising: aufstehen, ich stehe auf, stand auf, bin aufgestanden (comp. sep. verb). ² to tell. ³ purse. ⁴ to find: finden, fand, gefunden; habe: subj. mode after indirect speech, the pres. tense instead of impf. tense. ⁵ lost, verlieren, verlor, verloren (comp. insep. verb). ⁶ doch, yet. ⁷ noch, still.

3a. — Early Rising.

There is a proverb,¹ "Early to bed, early to rise, makes a man healthy, wealthy and wise²." A father once wished that his son, early in life,³ should understand⁴ the meaning⁵ of this proverb and practice⁶ it, and told him the following⁷: Two men went out⁸ one morning early and found a purse of gold. "But," said his hopeful⁹ son, "the person who lost this purse must¹⁰ have risen still earlier than those who found it." — The anecdote¹¹ does not tell¹² us what¹³ the father had to say.

¹ Sprichwort (n.). ² Morgenstunde hat Gold im Munde. ³ early in life, früh im Leben. ⁴ verstehen, verstand, verstanden (comp. insep. verb). ⁵ Bedeutung (f.). ⁶ üben (reg.). ⁷ Folgendes. ⁸ went out: ausgehen, gehe aus, ging aus, bin ausgegangen. ⁹ hoffnungsvoll (adj.). ¹⁰ müssen, ich muß, etc., pl. wir müssen, mußte, gemußt. ¹¹ Anekdote (f.). ¹² does not tell = tells us not, uns. ¹³ was (relative pronoun).

4. Die Welt[1] feben.

Ein Sohn sagte eines Tages zu seinem Vater, daß er herzlich[2] wünsche, die Welt zu sehen. Der Vater hörte[3] ihm mit großer Aufmerksamkeit[4] zu[5] und versetzte[6] dann: „Jch habe nichts dagegen,[6] daß du reisest, allein[7] ich fürchte,[8] daß die Welt dich sehen wird, während[9] du dieselbe[10] siehst."

world. [2] heartily. [3] zuhören, to listen to (dative). [4] attention. [5] to reply. [6] Jch habe nichts dagegen, I have nothing against it = no objection to. [7] allein, equivalent to aber. [8] to fear. [9] while. [10] the same, it (the world).

4a. — Seeing the World.

A certain[1] man had a son seventeen years old[2] who was rather[3] awkward.[4] One day this son said to his father that he would like to go travelling[5]; that he therefore would leave[6] home[7] for a time[8] in order to[9] see the world. His father, who had listened to[10] him with seeming[11] attention, replied: "I have no objection to your travelling (that you travel) to see the great world, but I fear very much[12] that the people of the world will see you while you see them[13]."

[1] Certain, gewiß (adj.). [2] a seventeen years old son, ein siebenzehn Jahre alter Sohn. [3] etwas. [4] unbeholfen. [5] he would like to go travelling, er möchte gern reisen, or auf Reisen gehen. [6] verlassen: du verläßt, verließ, verlassen (comp. insep. verb.). [7] Heimat. [8] für eine Zeit lang, or auf einige Zeit. [9] in order to, um ... zu (with infinitive). [10] to listen to, anhören (reg. comp. sep. verb, acc.). [11] scheinbar (adj.). [12] very much, sehr (the German adv. sehr modifies a verb as well as an adj. and adv.). [13] them, dieselben.

Answer in full in German the following questions:

Wessen Sohn wollte seine Heimat verlassen, und warum?

War der Vater zufrieden damit, daß sein Sohn auf Reisen gehen sollte?

Was fürchtete aber der Vater, im Fall (in case) sein Sohn sollte in die Welt gehen, um sie zu sehen?

5. Beſcheidene¹ Bitte.²

„Wollen Sie wohl ſo gefällig³ ſein, dieſen Rock bis an⁴ das Thor der nächſten Stadt mitzunehmen⁵?" bat⁶ ein junger Mann einen Herrn,⁷ der ihn in einem Wagen auf der Landſtraße⁸ ein= holte.⁹ „Mit vielem Vergnügen¹⁰," antwortete der Angeredete¹¹ ſehr freundlich; „wie wollen Sie ihn aber wieder bekommen¹²?" „O, das iſt leicht¹³ genug," entgegnete¹⁴ der Fußreiſende; „wenn Sie nichts dagegen haben, ſo bleibe¹⁵ ich darin¹⁶."

¹ modest. ² request. ³ kind, obliging. ⁴ bis an, as far as. ⁵ mitzu= nehmen (infin. with zu of mitnehmen: mit-zu-nehmen): ich nehme mit, du nimmſt mit, er nimmt mit, wir nehmen mit, etc.; nahm mit, mitgenommen, to take with you. ⁶ bitten, bat, gebeten, to request, to beg. ⁷ gentleman. ⁸ highway. ⁹ to overtake. ¹⁰ pleasure. ¹¹ a person addressed. ¹² to get again. ¹³ easy. ¹⁴ entgegnete, equivalent to antwortete. ¹⁵ to remain. ¹⁶ in it (therein).

5a. — A Modest Request.

It was a hot day, and a young man on foot[1] on[2] the way to a distant[3] city was very tired. He wished often he could[4] have a chance[5] to ride[6] with some one. So he frequently[7] looked[8] around, and at length[9] he saw a gentleman coming[10] behind him[11] in a carriage. This young man was naturally[12] a witty[13] fellow,[14] and he thought[15] he would[16] try[17] his wit[18] with this gentleman, who seemed[19] to be a friendly man, and who even[20] spoke[21] a few[22] words[23] to him. He asked this gentle- man then, if[24] he would[25] not be so kind[26] as[27] to take[28] his coat with him to the gate of the next city, which they could see in the distance.[29] "I will gladly do so[30]," said the gentle- man in the carriage, "but I cannot see how[31] you will get it again, unless[32] you can run[33] as fast[34] as my horse." "O," said the young wit,[35] "as to that,[36] that is easy enough; if you have no objection, I will remain in my coat." The gentleman thought the wit deserved[37] a reward,[38] and he took[39] him with him to[40] the city.

¹ ¾u Fuße. ² auf (dat. after a verb of rest). ³ entfernt. ⁴ könnte
(subj. mode, impf. tense of können). ⁵ Gelegenheit (f.). ⁶ to ride in a
carriage, fahren: ich fahre, fährst, fährt, fuhr, gefahren; to ride on a horse,
reiten, ritt, geritten. ⁷ häufig. ⁸ to look around, sich umsehen: ich sehe
mich um, du siehst dich um, er sieht sich um; sah mich um, mich umgesehen.
⁹ endlich. ¹⁰ coming (come, infin.), sah kommen. ¹¹ sich. ¹² von Natur.
¹³ witzig. ¹⁴ Bursche (m.), Geselle (m.). ¹⁵ to think, denken, dachte, gedacht.
¹⁶ wollen, wollte, gewollt; ich will, du willst, er will, infin. wollen. ¹⁷ versuchen (reg.). ¹⁸ Witz (m.); with, bei (dat.). ¹⁹ to seem, scheinen, schien,
geschienen. ²⁰ sogar. ²¹ to speak, sprechen: du sprichst, er spricht, sprach,
gesprochen. ²² einige. ²³ Wort (n, pl. Worte and Wörter, here Worte).
²⁴ ob. ²⁵ wollen. ²⁶ gut, or gütig. ²⁷ as to = to. ²⁸ See note 5, German
exercise 5. ²⁹ Entfernung, or Ferne (f.). ³⁰ gladly do so, es gern thun.
³¹ how, wie (relative conj. require the verb at the end). ³² unless, es sei
denn, daß (verb at the end). ³³ laufen, lief, gelaufen. ³⁴ schnell. ³⁵ wit,
Witzkopf, Witzling (f.). ³⁶ as to that, was das betrifft. ³⁷ verdienen (reg.
subj. pres. tense). ³⁸ Belohnung (f.). ³⁹ See note 5, on German exercise 5.
⁴⁰ in acc.

6. „Du verdienst¹ nicht, daß dich die Sonne bescheint²."

Ein Edelmann³ ging während großer Sonnenhitze⁴ in seinen
Garten und sah den Gärtner, welcher seinen Herrn nicht erwartet⁵
hatte, unter einem Baume schlafen. Zornig⁶ ging⁷ er auf ihn los
und rief⁸: „Schurke⁹! Du liegst¹⁰ hier, anstatt¹¹ zu arbeiten¹²;
du verdienst nicht, daß dich die Sonne bescheint." Der Gärtner
antwortete ruhig: „Ich weiß¹³ das, mein Herr¹⁴"; deshalb¹⁵ habe
ich mich in den Schatten gelegt¹⁶."

¹ to deserve. ² to shine upon. ³ nobleman. ⁴ heat of the sun. ⁵ to
expect. ⁶ angrily. ⁷ ging er auf ihn los; auf ihn losgehen; losgehen, gehe
los, ging los auf, bin losgegangen auf, to go up to, to go towards. ⁸ rufen,
rief, gerufen, to call, to cry out. ⁹ rascal, scoundrel. ¹⁰ liegen, lag, gelegen, to lie. ¹¹ instead of. ¹² to work, working. ¹³ wissen: ich weiß, etc.,
wir wissen, wußte, gewußt, to know, to be aware of it. ¹⁴ sir. ¹⁵ therefore, on that account. ¹⁶ to lie down.

6a.—"You do not deserve to have the Sun shine upon you."

It was a hot day, and a nobleman went into the garden
which he had behind¹ his large house. There² he saw his

gardener lying in the shade of a tree. The nobleman was angry and went to his gardener under the tree, woke[3] him and said: "You rascal, you are asleep here instead of working in the garden; you do not deserve to have the sun shine upon you." The gardener then sat up,[4] looked[5] at his master, and replied coolly: "I know it, sir, and so[6] I went into the shade."

[1] hinter (dative after a verb of rest). [2] Da, dort. [3] wecken (reg. acc.). [4] sich aufrichten: ich richte mich auf (reg.). [5] to look at, ansehen: ich sehe an, sah an, angesehen (acc.). [6] and so, und so, or und also.

---

7. Freunde am Hofe.[1]

Ein Landmann trieb[2] eines Tages[3] einen Esel durch eine Stadt und schlug[4] ihn sehr oft. Ein Herr kam gerade[5] dann aus seinem Hause und schalt[6] den Eseltreiber,[7] weil er sein Thier so grausam[8] behandelte,[9] und sagte: „Hören Sie auf,[10] Schurke, sonst[11] werde ich Sie peitschen[12] lassen[13]!" Der Eseltreiber entgegnete[14]: „Ich bitte um Verzeihung,[15] guter Herr; es freut[16] mich, daß mein Esel Freunde am Hofe hat."

[1] at court. [2] treiben, trieb, getrieben, to drive. [3] one day (genitive of indefinite time). [4] schlagen: du schlägst, er schlägt, schlug, geschlagen, to beat. [5] just. [6] schelten, schalt, gescholten, to scold, to berate. [7] muleteer. [8] cruelly. [9] behandeln (reg.), to use, treat. [10] aufhören, to stop, to cease. [11] else. [12] peitschen (reg.), to whip. [13] lassen: du lässest, er läßt, ließ, gelassen, to let; here "to have" (the English verb "to have" with a past part., meaning "to allow, or cause to be done," is in German translated lassen, — as: I have a coat made, ich lasse einen Rock machen — followed by the infinitive). [14] The same as antwortete. [15] I beg your pardon. [16] es freut mich, or ich freue mich, I am pleased.

7a.—Friends at Court.

A countryman drove a donkey through the streets of a city. This donkey was laden[1] with two heavy[2] bags,[3] and, like[4] all donkeys, was walking[5] very slowly,[6] and his master often beat him unmercifully. As the countryman was again beating his donkey, he was just[7] before[8] the door of a gentleman, who came out of the house and saw [9] it. He at once [10] reproved [11] the countryman for it, [12] and said to him : " Stop, you rascal, or I will have you whipped as you whip your poor beast [13] !" The countryman thought he knew his business [14] and answered : " I beg your pardon, sir ; I am pleased to hear that my poor donkey has friends at court."

[1] laden, belaben, belub, belaben. [2] ſchwer. [3] Sađ (m., pl. Sâđe). [4] wie. [5] was walking, walked: gehen. [6] langſam. [7] eben, gerabe. [8] vor (dative after verb of rest). [9] and who saw it (relative understood, must have the verb at the end). [10] ſogleich. [11] ſchelten. [12] beswegen. [13] Tier (n.). [14] Geſchäft (f.), Angelegenheit (f.).

8. Die Erwiberung [1] eines Matroſen. [2]

Ein Mann ſagte zu einem Matroſen, ber ſich eben auf eine lange Seereiſe [3] einſchiffen [4] wollte : „Ich wunbre [5] mich, baß du bich noch auf baß Meer [6] wagſt [7]; ba boch [8] bein Vater, Großvater unb Urgroßvater alle auf bem Waſſer geſtorben [9] ſinb." „Lieber Freunb," fragte ber Matroſe, „wo ſtarb benn bein Vater ?" „Im Bett, wie alle ſeine Vorfahren [10] vor ihm," war beſſen [11] Antwort. „Dann wunbert eß auch mich, baß bu bich noch inß Bett wagſt, ba boch bein Vater, Großvater unb Urgroßvater barin geſtorben ſinb," bemerkte [12] ber Matroſe.

[1] retort. [2] sailor. [3] voyage. [4] to embark, to go on board. [5] to wonder. [6] sea. [7] to venture. [8] since indeed. [9] ſterben: bu ſtirbſt, er ſtirbt, ſtarb, iſt geſtorben. [10] ancestors. [11] his. [12] to remark, to observe.

8a. — A Sailor's Retort.

A merchant met [1] a sailor, and had a conversation [2] with him. Among other things [3] he asked him where his father died. The sailor answered : " My father, my grandfather and great-grand-father all died on the sea." " And are you not afraid [4] to go upon the water?" asked the merchant again. The sailor replied to this [5] : " Will you tell me, please, [6] where your ancestors died?" " They all died in their beds," said the merchant, "like good christians[7]." "Now then[8]," said the sailor, "your ancestors all died in bed, and you are not afraid to go to bed, and am I to[9] be afraid to go to sea, because[10] my ancestors died there?"

[1] to meet, begegnen (reg., comp. ins. verb dative). [2] Unterhaltung (f.). [3] among other things, unter anderen Dingen, unter anderem. [4] sich fürchten: ich fürchte mich, du fürchtest dich, er fürchtet sich (reg.). [5] to this, darauf. [6] please, gefälligst. [7] Christ (m., pl. –en). [8] now then, nun. [9] I am to, ich soll (as: I am to go to Boston, ich soll nach Boston gehen; somebody desires me to go). [10] weil (subord. conj.).

---

9. Der Franzose[1] in England.

Ein Franzose begegnete[2] einem englischen Soldaten mit der Waterloo=Medaille,[3] und tadelte[4] die englische Regierung, daß sie eine solche[5] Kleinigkeit[6] verleihe,[7] die keine drei Franken koste.[8] „Das ist freilich wahr[9]," erwiderte der Held[10]; „aber sie[11] kostet der französischen Regierung einen Napoleon[12]."

[1] Frenchman. [2] See note 1, English exercise 8. [3] medal. [4] to blame, to find fault with. [5] eine solche, such a. [6] trifle. [7] verleihen, verlieh, verliehen; verleihe (subj. mood after indirect speech =) to bestow. [8] to cost (subj. mood as in note 7). [9] Das ist freilich wahr, to be sure, I admit. [10] hero. [11] sie, she (here the medal = it). [12] Napoleon is a gold coin worth about $4.00; but the word is used here as pun, and refers to Napoleon I.

9a. — The Frenchman in England.

A Frenchman was once travelling[1] in England. Here, among other strangers,[2] he met an English soldier, who had on his breast[3] a medal in memory[4] of the battle[5] of[6] Waterloo. The Frenchman, a little vexed,[7] sneered[8] at the English government for bestowing[9] such a trifle, that was not worth three francs. The Englishman, proud[10] of the honor[11] of the medal, and ready[12] with a retort, replied coolly: "It may[13] be as you say in regard[14] to the value[15]; I am not certain. But what I (do) know for[16] certain is, that it cost the French government a

Napoleon." The words of the Englishman have, as may easily be seen,[17] a double [18] meaning ; but, very likely,[19] the Frenchman took that[20] which concerned [21] him. At least [22] we hear [23] of no reply [24] from [25] him.

[1] was travelling, travelled: reifen (reg.). [2] Frembe (m., pl. –n)., [3] Bruft (f.). [4] in memory of, zur Erinnerung an (acc.). [5] Schlacht (f.). [6] bei. [7] a little vexed, ein wenig ärgerlich. [8] to sneer at, verfpotten (reg.). [9] for bestowing, that it bestowed. [10] proud of, ftolz auf (acc.). [11] Ehre (f.). [12] ready with, bereit mit, or bei der Hand mit. [13] It may, das mag. [14] in regard to, in Bezug auf (acc.). [15] Wert (m.). [16] für. [17] as may easily be seen, wie leicht zu fehen ift. [18] boppelt (adj.). [19] very likely, fehr wahrfcheinlich. [20] die (fem., referring to "meaning"; a fem. in German). [21] betreffen, es betrifft, betraf, betroffen (acc.). [22] wenigftens. [23] to hear of, hören von (dat.). [24] Antwort (f.). [25] von ihm.

10. Zwei Maler.[1]

Ein ärmlicher[2] Künftler,[3] der fich für[4] einen großen Maler hielt,[5] fprach[6] eines Tages zu einem anberen Maler bavon,[6] die Decke[4] feines Saales[7] zu bemalen.[8] „Ich weiße[9] fie erft[10]," fagte er, „unb bann werbe ich fie malen." „Ich benke," fagte fein Freunb, der ein Schelm[11] war, „es wäre[12] beffer, Sie malten biefelbe[13] erft unb weißten fie bann."

[1] painter. [2] poor, wretched. [3] artist. [4] fich halten für: ich halte mich, bu hältft, er hält, hielt, gehalten, to think one's self. [5] fprechen: bu fprichft, er fpricht, fprach, gefprochen; bavon fprechen, to speak of it = spoke of painting. [6] ceiling. [7] hall. [8] to paint. [9] to whitewash. [10] first. [11] rogue. [12] would be. [13] the same, it.

10a. — Two Painters.

There was once a man who thought he was [1] a great painter. One day he wished to paint his hall very beautifully. He spoke to another painter of it, and also told him what[2] beautiful sceneries[3] he would[4] paint on[5] the ceiling. "First," said he, " I shall whitewash it as nicely [6] as possible,[7] and then paint it." His friend, who was a great artist as well as a wit,[8] answered mischievously[9]: "Allow[10] me to give you a good advice[11]: You had better paint it first,[12] and then whitewash it[13]."

[1] was, wäre (subj. mood, in indirect speech after think = denken). [2] what, what kind of, was für. [3] Landschaften (pl.). [4] wollte (impf. tense of wollen). [5] auf (acc. of the verb of motion. [6] hübsch, neat. [7] möglich. [8] as well as a wit, sowohl als auch ein Witzkopf, or als auch, etc. [9] schadenfroh, boshaft, schelmisch. [10] erlauben (reg.). [11] Rat. [12] you had better paint it first, malen Sie dieselbe lieber erst. [13] it, es (here referring to the fem. noun Decke; sie, she).

Beantworten Sie auf Deutsch die folgenden Fragen:

Was dachte dieser Mann in der Anekdote von sich selbst?

Welchen Rat gab ihm ein anderer Maler?

Welcher von diesen zwei Männern hätte die Decke schöner malen können (hätte malen können, could have painted), der Erstere oder der Letztere?

11. Die Spornen[1] verbrennen.[2]

Als ein Reisender in einer sehr kalten Nacht in die Küche[3] eines Wirtshauses[4] kam, stand[5] er so nahe bei[6] dem Feuer, daß er seine Stiefel[7] verbrannte. Ein Mann, welcher in einer Ecke[8] saß,[9] rief ihm zu[10]: „Mein Herr, Sie werden gleich[11] Ihre Spornen verbrennen." „Sie meinen vermutlich[12] meine Stiefel," sagte der Herr. „Nein," erwiderte der Andere, „diese[13] sind schon verbrannt."

[1] Spurs. [2] verbrennen, verbrannte, verbrannt, to burn, to spoil by burning, or to consume by fire. [3] kitchen. [4] inn. [5] stehen, stand, gestanden. [6] so nahe bei, so near (to). [7] boot. [8] corner. [9] sitzen, saß, gesessen, to sit, to be sitting. [10] zurufen: rief zu, zugerufen (dat.). [11] soon, directly. [12] probably, very likely. [13] diese, these (the demonstrative pronoun often stands in German for the personal pronoun, as here = they).

11a. — Burning the Spurs.

It was a cold night. It was snowing[1] fast,[2] and the wind blew.[3] A traveller came to a country-inn[4] late that night,[5] and

as his boots were wet,⁶ and his feet cold, he went into the
warmest⁷ room⁸ of the house, the kitchen. There was a large
fireplace⁹ there, and a good fire in it.¹⁰ He now¹¹ wanted¹² to
warm¹³ his feet; but as he stood too¹⁴ near the fire, he burned
his boots. When a man, who was sitting in a corner, saw it, he
said after a while¹⁵: "Sir, you will soon burn your spurs." The
traveller, not believing¹⁶ what this man said, replied: "You
mean probably my boots," for¹⁷ he did not think it possible¹⁸
that his steel¹⁹ spurs could burn. Upon this²⁰ the man in the
corner answered coolly: "Oh no, sir, I mean what I say, for
your boots were²¹ burned some time ago²²."

¹ it was snowing, it snowed, ſchneien (reg.). ² ſtark. ³ blaſen, blies,
geblaſen, or gehen. ⁴ Landwirtshaus (n.). ⁵ that night, in that night, in
jener Nacht (fem. noun of time use generally a preposition to form adver-
bial expressions. ⁶ naß. ⁷ warm, comp. wärmer, sup. wärmſt (adj. of
one syllable modify the root-vowel, if the vowel can be modified in forming the degrees of comparison, with some exceptions). ⁸ Zimmer (n.).
Feuerplatz (a coined word). ¹⁰ darin. ¹¹ he now wanted = he wanted
now, nun. ¹² wollte. ¹³ wärmen. ¹⁴ zu. ¹⁵ after a while, nach einer
Weile, nach einiger Zeit. ¹⁶ not believing, who believed not. ¹⁷ for,
denn (a coordinate conj., no change of construction). ¹⁸ he did not think
it possible, er hielt es nicht für möglich. ¹⁹ Stahl (m.). ²⁰ darauf. ²¹ were,
are (pres. tense). ²² some time ago, ſchon lange.

---

12. General Waſhington.

Der berühmte¹ General Georg Waſhington ſaß einmal mit
mehreren² ſeiner Offiziere³ bei Tiſche.⁴ Da ſtieß⁵ einer von ihnen
einen Fluch⁶ aus.⁵ Waſhington ließ⁷ Meſſer und Gabel fallen,⁷
warf⁸ einen ſtrengen⁹ Blick¹⁰ auf den Flucher,¹¹ ſo daß dieſer die
Augen¹² niederſchlug.¹³ Waſhington ſagte dann: „Ich hätte
geglaubt,¹⁴ wir alle betrachteten¹⁵ uns ſelbſt als anſtändige¹⁶
Männer."

¹ famous, renowned, celebrated. ² several. ³ officer. ⁴ bei Tiſche, at
the table, at dinner. ⁵ ausſtoßen: du ſtößeſt, er ſtößt, ſtieß aus, ausge-
ſtoßen, to utter. ⁶ curse. ⁷ ließ fallen, let fall, to drop. ⁸ werfen: du

wirfſt, er wirft, warf, geworfen, to throw. [9] severe. [10] look. [11] curser.
[12] eye. [13] niederſchlug, ſchlägſt, ſchlägt, ſchlug nieder, niedergeſchlagen, to
cast down. [14] ich hätte geglaubt (subj. mode, plupf. tense, instead of
second conditional, "I should have thought." [15] to consider. [16] respectable.

12a. — General Washington.

The father of his country, General George Washington, was
sitting (sat) once at dinner[1] with a number[2] of his officers, when
one of them uttered an oath.   As Washington heard this, he
laid[3] knife and fork on[4] the table, and cast a reproving[5] glance[6]
at[7] the swearer.   The guilty[8] officer noticed[9] it, and cast down
his eyes with shame.[10]   After a while Washington said : "I
thought we were[11] all respectable men."

[One would[12] think that Washington's example[13] would bear[14]
good fruit[15]; but, alas,[16] that is not the case.[17]   On the contrary,[18] common[19] people in America swear a great deal[20]; and
not only[21] men, but also[21] boys[23] we hear swear.   And what is
indeed[23] worse than to hear a little fellow[24] utter a great[25] oath !]

[1] zu Tiſche, beim Mittagseſſen. [2] Anzahl (f.). [3] legen (reg.). [4] auf
(acc. verb of motion; when the English preposition "on" has the meaning of "upon," the German is auf). [5] tabelnd (adj.). [6] Blick (m.). [7] auf
(acc.). [8] ſchuldig (adj.). [9] bemerken (reg.). [10] vor Scham. [11] were (subj.
mode after "thought," denken. [12] man ſollte. [13] Beiſpiel (n.). [14] tragen,
trägſt, trägt, trug, getragen. [15] Frucht (f., pl. Früchte). [16] leider. [17] Fall
(m.). [18] on the contrary, im Gegenteil. [19] gewöhnlich. [20] a great deal,
much, viel. [21] not only . . . but also, nicht nur . . . ſondern auch. [22] in
der That. [23] ſchlimmer. [24] Burſche (m., pl. –n). [25] ſchwer.

---

13. Das Kalb[1] ein wenig[2] halten.[3]

Lord Abington ging eines Tages durch ein Dorf[4] und begegnete
einem Knaben, der ein Kalb mit ſich führte,[5] und welcher, als der
Lord an ihn herankam,[6] ſtehen blieb[7] und ihn mit offenem Munde
anſchaute.[8]   Der Lord fragte den Knaben, ob er ihn kenne.[9]   Dieſer
antwortete „Ja."   „Wie heiße ich denn," ſagte der Lord dann.

„Lord Abington," antwortete der Knabe. „Warum[10] nimmst[11] du
also[12] deinen Hut nicht ab?" fragte der Lord wieder.[13] „Das will
ich gern thun,[14] mein Herr," antwortete der Knabe, „wenn Sie das
Kalb ein wenig halten wollen."

[1] calf. [2] a little, a little while. [3] halten, hältst, hält, hielt, gehalten, to
to hold. [4] village. [5] mit sich führen, to lead (with one's self). [6] herankommen, komme heran, an ihn herankommen, to come near him, to
approach. [7] stehen bleiben, blieb; stehen geblieben, ich bin, to remain
standing, to stop. [8] anschauen, to look at, to gaze at. [9] kennen, kannte,
gekannt, to know, to be acquainted (kenne, subj. mode of present tense,
for past tense [which often occurs] after ob in indirect questions). [10] why.
[11] abnehmen, to take off. [12] then. [13] again. [14] thun, that, gethan, to do.

13a. — Holding the Calf a Minute.

A certain Lord Abington, an Englishman, was one day on a
short[1] journey, and came through a village. Here he met a
boy who was leading a calf. This boy stopped on the road[2]
and stared at the lord with open mouth, when he came near
him. When the lord noticed the boy, he also stopped, and
asked him if he knew[3] him. The boy then answered "Yes,"
and the gentleman asked him what his name was.[4] The boy
with the calf gave[5] his name.[6] Then the lord questioned[7] him
once more[8]: "Why do you not take off your hat?" The boy
replied coolly, he would gladly do that, if Lord Abington would
hold his calf a minute.

[1] kurz. [2] Landstraße (f.); Straße (f.); Weg (m.). [3] kennen (present
tense, subj. mode to be used). [4] heißen, hieß, geheißen (use subj. mode,
present tense). [5] geben, giebst, giebt, gab, gegeben. [6] Name (m.). [7] to
question, to ask. [8] once more, noch einmal.

---

14. Die goldene[1] Gans.[2]

Die Königin von Hannover kehrte[3] auf einer Reise in einem
Wirtshause ein,[3] „Die goldene Gans" genannt,[4] wo sie für drei
Tage dreihundert Thaler bezahlen[5] mußte. Der Wirt[6] ersuchte[7]

fie beim Einſteigen⁸ in den Wagen unterthänigſt,⁹ ihm bei ihrer
Rückkehr¹⁰ wieder die Ehre ihres Beſuchs¹¹ zu gönnen.¹² „Wenn
Sie wollen, daß ich das thun ſoll, mein lieber Herr, ſo müſſen¹³
Sie mich nicht wieder für Ihr Schild¹⁴ halten¹⁵,“ antwortete die
Königin freundlich.¹⁶

¹ golden. ² goose. ³ einkehren, to alight. ⁴ nennen, nannte, genannt,
to call, to name. ⁵ to pay. ⁶ host, landlord. ⁷ to request. ⁸ beim Ein=
ſteigen, on entering. ⁹ humbly. ¹⁰ on her return. ¹¹ visit. ¹² to grant.
¹³ müſſen: ich muß, du mußt, er muß, wir müſſen, etc., mußte, gemußt,
must, to be obliged (as in English, the verb following is used without zu
in German). ¹⁴ sign. ¹⁵ halten für, to take for. ¹⁶ good-naturedly.

14a.—The Golden Goose.

When the queen of Hanover was once on a journey, she
alighted¹ at a country-inn. It is customary² for almost³ all the
inns in the old world to have⁴ a name (for example⁵: "The
Lion⁶," "The Star⁷," "The Sun⁸," "The Moon⁹," "The
Bear¹⁰," etc.¹¹). This was called¹² "The Golden Goose." The
weather being pleasant,¹³ and the surroundings¹⁴ charming,¹⁵
she stayed¹⁶ three days. When she was about¹⁷ to depart,¹⁸ the
landlord sent¹⁹ up a bill²⁰ of $300. She paid it without find-
ing fault²¹ with it.²² He saw²³ her then to²⁴ her carriage, and
requested her, with the greatest humility,²⁵ to favor him again
with a visit on her return. She replied good-naturedly²⁶: "If
you want²⁷ me to do that, you must not take me again for your
sign."

¹ einkehren. ² gebräuchlich. ³ faſt, beinahe. ⁴ for "almost," "to have,"
"that almost all have." ⁵ for example, zum Beiſpiel (usually abridged
z. B.). ⁶ Löwe (m.). ⁷ Stern (m.). ⁸ Sonne (f.). ⁹ Mond (m.). ¹⁰ Bär
(m., pl. -en). ¹¹ etc., und ſo weiter (usually abridged u. ſ. w.).
¹² to be called: heißen, hieß, geheißen. ¹³ being pleasant (this pres. part.
is best translated by a conj., as: since the weather, etc., da, etc.; pleasant
= angenehm). ¹⁴ Umgebung (f., use sing.). ¹⁵ reizend. ¹⁶ bleiben (to
remain). ¹⁷ to be about = im Begriff ſein, zu; ich bin im Begriff. ¹⁸ to
depart, abzureiſen. ¹⁹ to send up, hinaufſchicken (reg.). ²⁰ Rechnung (f.).
²¹ without finding fault, ohne ſich zu beklagen. ²² with it, darüber. ²³ to
see to = begleiten (reg.) bis. ²⁴ an (acc.). ²⁵ Demut (f.). ²⁶ gutmütig,
freundlich). ²⁷ want me, want that I should do that.

15. Wieder jung werden.[1]

Ein kleines fünf Jahre[2] altes Mädchen[3] liebte[4] ihre Mutter und Großmutter gleich sehr.[5] An dem Geburtstage[6] der letztern[7] sagte ihre Mutter zu ihr: „Mein liebes Kind, du mußt Gott bitten,[8] daß er deine Großmutter segne,[9] und daß sie sehr alt werden möge.[10] Das Kind sah seine Mutter mit einigem[11] Erstaunen[12] an. Die Mutter, welche den Blick bemerkte, sagte: „Nun, willst du nicht Gott bitten, daß deine Großmutter sehr alt werde[13]?" „Ach, Mutter," sagte das Kind, „sie ist schon alt, ich will lieber beten, daß sie wieder jung werde.[13]"

[1] werden, wirst, wird, wurde, geworden, to become, to grow. [2] year.
[3] girl. [4] to love. [5] gleich sehr, equally well. [6] birthday. [7] the latter.
[8] bitten, bat, gebeten, to ask, to beg, to pray to. [9] segnen (reg. segne; subj. mode of the pres. tense after the verb bitten), to bless. [10] mögen: ich mag, etc., mochte, gemocht (möge, subj. mode of pres. tense; see note 9).
[11] some. [12] surprise. [13] Subj. mode after the verbs bitten and beten.

15a. — Becoming Young Again.

A lady had a little daughter about five years old, who loved her mother and grandmother equally well. On the birthday of the latter, the mother asked[1] her little daughter Emma (that[2] was her name[3]) to pray to God that he would bless her grandmother, and that she might become very old. Her grandmother was quite[4] old already,[5] and the little girl knew[6] enough to see it. She therefore[7] looked at her mother with surprise at this request.[8] The mother noticed the look of her child, and asked again: "Well,[9] will you not pray to God that your grandmother may become older?" The little girl answered with childlike[10] simplicity[11]: "Dear mother, grandma is already very old, I would rather pray to God that she may become young again."

[1] bitten, bat, gebeten. [2] so. [3] heißen. [4] ziemlich. [5] schon. [6] wissen.
[7] daher. [8] at this request, bei diesem Ersuchen. [9] nun. [10] kindlich. [11] Einfalt (f.), Unschuld (f.), innocence.

16. „Sein oder nicht sein.‟

Ein Schauspieler[1] wandte[2] sich an den Direktor[3] Quin, um[4] auf dessen[5] Bühne[6] zugelassen[7] zu werden,[8] und begann[9] den berühmten Monolog[10] aus Hamlet: „Sein oder nicht sein, das ist die Frage[11].‟ Dieser alberne[12] Vortrag[13] mißfiel[14] Quin so sehr, daß er ausrief[15]: „Auf Ehre, das ist keine Frage; ganz[16] gewiß[16] nicht sein.‟

[1] Actor. [2] sich wenden, wandte mich, ich habe mich gewandt; at times gewendet = to apply, make application to. [3] manager. [4] um...zu, in order to. [5] dessen = whose, of whom, his. [6] stage. [7] zulassen, lasse zu, ließ zu, zugelassen, to admit. [8] Passive voice. [9] beginnen, begann, begonnen, to begin. [10] soliloquy. [11] question. [12] absurd, simple. [13] delivery, recital. [14] mißfallen, mißfällst, mißfiel, mißfallen, to displease. [15] ausrufen, rief aus, ausgerufen, to cry out. [16] ganz gewiß, most certainly.

16a. — "To be or not to be."

It once happened[1] that an actor came to London in order to obtain[2] a situation[3] in[4] one of the London[5] theaters. He therefore went to Mr. Quin, at that time[6] stage-manager of the far-famed[7] Drury Lane Theater. In order to give this gentleman a specimen[8] of his ability[9] as a dramatic[10] actor, he declaimed[11] the famous soliloquy from Shakespeare's Hamlet: "To be or not to be, that is the question." The applicant[12] delivered[13] this fine passage[14] absurdly enough, and the manager, himself[15] a famous dramatic actor, and an expert[16] in[17] such things, stopped[18] him in the same[19] strain[20]: "There can be no question; most certainly not to be."

[1] geschehen, geschieht, geschah, geschehen (impersonal verb). [2] zu erlangen (reg.). [3] Anstellung (f.), Stelle (f.). [4] auf. [5] Londoner (adj. indeclinable. — Adjectives of proper names, of cities, towns and countries, are often formed by adding er to the name, and are not declined). [6] zur Zeit. [7] weit berühmt. [8] Probe (f.). [9] Fähigkeit (f.). [10] als ein dramatischer. [11] deklamieren (reg.; past part. deklamiert, not gedeklamiert). [12] Bewerber (m.). [13] vortragen: trägst, trägt vor, trug vor, vorgetragen. [14] Stelle (f.). [15] selbst. [16] Kenner (m.). [17] von (dat.). [18] to stop, to interrupt, unterbrechen, unterbrichst, unterbricht, unterbrach, unterbrochen. [19] der-, die-, dasselbe. [20] Ton (m.), or Zug (m.).

Beantworten Sie bie folgenben Fragen auf Deutſch :

Wer kam nach London, unb was wollte er ba?

Zu wem ging bieſer Schauſpieler, um eine Anſtellung zu erlangen?

Welche Stellung hatte Quin zu jener Zeit?

Was that bieſer Schauſpieler, um bem Direktor eine Probe
ſeiner Fähigkeit zu geben?

War ber Direktor mit ber Deklamation bes Bewerbers zufrieben?

17. Der Reiſende[1] unb der Schiffer.[2]

Ein Reiſenber kam an einen Fluß[3] unb mietete[4] ein Boot, um
ihn überzuſetzen.[5] Da bas Waſſer ein wenig bewegter[6] war, als
ihm gefiel,[7] ſo fragte er ben Schiffer, ob jemanb bei bieſer Über-
fahrt[8] verloren worben wäre.[9] „Niemals[10]," erwiberte ber Schiffer,
„niemals! Mein Bruber ertrank[11] hier letzte Woche,[12] aber wir
fanben ihn am nächſten Tage wieber."

[1] Reiſenbe, traveller (is an adj., and is declined like one, as : ber Reiſenbe, ein Reiſenber). [2] boatman. [3] river. [4] to hire. [5] to ferry him
across. [6] rough. [7] gefallen, es gefällt mir, gefiel, es hat mir gefallen = to
please. [8] passage. [9] verlieren, verlor, verloren; worben wäre (subj. mode
of plupf. tense of werben forming passive voice; subj. mode after indirect
question = "had been lost"). [10] never. [11] ertrinken, ertrank, ertrunken,
to be drowned. [12] week.

17a. — The Traveller and the Boatman.

A man was once on a journey, and came to a river, across[1]
which (there) was no bridge[2]; neither[3] was the water frozen,[4] as it
was in summer. He had[5] to hire a boat, therefore, to take (ferry)
him across. The weather was quite windy,[6] and consequently[7]
the water rougher than he liked. As he had not often been on
the water, he was a little frightened,[8] and asked the boatman,
if (there) were (any) danger[9] at such times,[10] and if anybody
had ever been lost on this passage. The sailor, a man of few
words,[11] and one[12] who took everything literally,[13] answered

quietly: "Never lost, sir, never! It is true,[14] my brother was drowned here last month,[15] but we found him the day after[16]."

[1] über (prepos., acc.). [2] Brücke (f.). [3] auch .. nicht. [4] gefrieren, gefror, gefroren. [5] had, was obliged, müffen. [6] windig. [7] folglich. [8] erfchrecken, erfchrack, erfchrocken. [9] Gefahr (f.). [10] zu folchen Zeiten. [11] of few words, von wenig Worten. [12] einer. [13] wörtlich; buchftäblich. [14] zwar. [15] Monat (m., acc. definite time). [16] nachher.

---

18. Der Schulmonarch.

Als Karl der Zweite den Doktor Busby befuchte,[1] foll[2] der Doktor, den Hut auf dem Kopfe,[3] durch die Schule gegangen fein, während[4] Se.[5] Majeftät, den Hut in der Hand, hinter ihm her=fchritt.[6] Als der König aber an der Thüre Abfchied[7] nahm, redete[8] ihn der Doktor mit großer Demut fo[9] an[8]: „Sire, ich hoffe,[10] Ew.[11] Majeftät werden[12] meinen Mangel[13] an Refpekt entfchuldi=gen[14]; denn, wenn meine Knaben wüßten,[15] daß es einen größeren Mann im Reiche[16] gäbe[17] als ich, fo würde ich nie im Stande[18] fein, fie zu regieren[19]."

[1] to visit. [2] follen is used here in the meaning of "is said or reported to be" (follen can, in this sense, be used only in the pres. tense; the following verb may stand in the past, as: er foll angekommen fein, he is said to have arrived). [3] his head. [4] while. [5] His. [6] herfchreiten, fchritt her, hergefchritten, to stride, to step, to walk, to walk on behind him. [7] leave (farewell). [8] anreden, ich rede an, to address. [9] thus. [10] to hope. [11] your. [12] werden after the subj. in the singular. — Princes are addressed in the plural in court language. [13] Mangel an, want of. [14] excuse. [15] wüß=ten (subj. mode of imperf. tense after wenn, "if," conditionally). [16] realm, kingdom. [17] gäbe, subj. mode, impf. tense of geben (es giebt, "there is," used when no small, distinct place is mentioned; the English nominative is in German in the acc., as: es giebt einen Mann, there is a man. [18] im Stande fein, to be able. [19] to govern, to rule.

18a. — The School Monarch.

It happened one day that Charles II. (the second) visited a school. The master (principal) of the school, a certain Dr.

Busby, went with His Majesty through all the rooms, of which [1]
there was a great number. As they were going through the
various [2] rooms, the monarch, as it is becoming [3] for any [4] man
to do, took off his hat, while the master kept [5] his on his head.
When the king was on the point [6] of going, [7] the master went
with him as far as the door, and said to him with the greatest
humility, he hoped [8] His Majesty would [9] excuse his want of
respect ; but if these boys knew that there was a greater man in
the kingdom than he, he should no longer be able to govern
them, and they would surely [10] drive him out of the school-house.

[1] beren, or von benen. [2] verſchieben. [3] it is becoming, es ſchickt ſich. [4] it
is becoming for any man to do, es ſchickt ſich für Jedermann. [5] kept his
on his head, kept his on, behielt ſeinen auf. [6] to be on the point, im
Begriff ſein. [7] to go. [8] All the following verbs must be in subj. mode,
impf. tense, after indirect speech. [9] würde, möchte. [10] ſicherlich. .

19. Das Fragezeichen. [1]

Pope, von Natur klein und verwachſen, [2] war mit einigen Freun=
ben in einem Kaffeehauſe und ſtritt [3] ſich mit ihnen über [4] den Sinn [5]
einer lateiniſchen Stelle. [6] Ein junger Herr, der in der Nähe [7]
ſtand, bat [8] höflich [9] um [8] das Blatt. [10] Pope reichte [11] es ihm mit
wegwerfendem [12] Blick hin. [13] Nach aufmerkſamem [13] Durchleſen [14]
gab jener das Blatt zurück und ſagte, er glaubte, baß, um es ver=
ſtändlich [15] zu machen, nach einem gewiſſen Worte ein Fragezeichen
ſtehen [16] ſollte. Pope, ärgerlich, [17] baß der Fehler [18] ſeinem Scharf=
blick [19] entgangen [20] war, warf [21] bem jungen Mann die ſpitzige [22]
Frage hin: „Was iſt ein Fragezeichen?" Schnell, aber kalt,
erwiderte dieſer: „Ein kleines, buckliges Ding, das oft unver=
ſchämt [23] fragt."

[1] interrogation-point. [2] deformed. [3] ſich ſtreiten, ſtritt, geſtritten.
[4] about. [5] meaning, sense. [6] passage. [7] near by. [8] bitten, bat, gebe=
ten, bitten um, to ask for. [9] politely. [10] paper (leaf). [11] hinreichen
(reg.), to hand. [12] disdainful. [13] careful. [14] perusal. [15] clear, plain.

¹⁶ ſtehen, ſtand, geſtanden, to stand. ¹⁷ vexed. ¹⁸ mistake. ¹⁹ scrutiny.
²⁰ entgehen, entging, iſt entgangen, to escape. ²¹ hinwerfen, warf hin, hin=
geworfen, to dart. ²² sharp, spiteful. ²³ impudently.

19a. — The Interrogation-Point.

All the contemporaries[1] of the great English poet, Pope, tell
us that he was very plain-featured,[2] deformed, and very small in
stature.[3] One evening he was sitting with some friends in a
coffee-house, and they were deeply engaged[4] in conversation[5]
about a learned subject.[6] Among other things, they were dis-
puting about the meaning of a Latin passage, and could not
agree.[7] A young man, who stood near, had listened[8] to their
opinions,[9] and after a time politely asked for the paper. Pope
handed it to him with a disdainful glance. After the young
man had read the manuscript[10] very carefully, he handed it
back, and remarked that he thought, to make it intelligible, an
interrogation-point should stand after a certain word. Pope,
vexed that the omission[11] of this important[12] punctuation[13] had
escaped his scrutiny, darted this spiteful question at the young
man: "What is an interrogation-point?" Quickly, but coolly,
the young man replied: "A small, crooked thing that asks
questions[14]."

[1] Zeitgenoſſe (m., pl. -en). [2] einfach von Ausſehen, häßlich. [3] von Kör=
per, von Statur. [4] vertieft. [5] in Unterhaltung. [6] ein gelehrter Gegen=
ſtand. [7] to agree, einig werden. [8] to listen to, zuhören (sep. verb; reg.,
dative). [9] Meinung (f.). [10] Handſchrift (f.). [11] Auslaſſung (f.). [12] wich=
tig. [13] Interpunktion (f.). [14] to ask a question, eine Frage ſtellen, fragen.

---

20. Die gefundene[1] Brille.[2]

Ein Herr von einer Bibelgeſellſchaft,[3] welcher eine alte Frau
beſuchte, um zu ſehen, ob ſie eine Bibel habe,[4] wurde mit der fol=
genden Antwort hart[5] getadelt[6]: „Glauben Sie, mein Herr, daß
ich eine Heidin[7] bin, daß Sie eine ſolche Frage an mich richten[8]?
Geh',“ ſagte ſie dann zu einem kleinen Mädchen, „und hole[9] meine

Bibel aus meiner Schublade,[10] daß ich sie diesem Herrn zeige[11]."
Die Bibel, sorgfältig[12] in Papier eingeschlagen,[13] um den Einband[14]
zu schonen,[15] wurde gebracht.[16] Beim Öffnen[17] derselben[18] rief die
alte Frau aus: „Ei, wie froh bin ich, daß Sie gekommen sind . . .
Hier ist meine Brille, die ich schon seit zwei Jahren suche,[19] und
wußte nicht, wo ich sie finden sollte."

[1] finden, fand, gefunden, to find (an adj. here, formed from a past part.).
[2] Brille, (f., a singular in German), spectacles. [3] Bible-society. [4] habe
(subj. mode of pres. tense, instead of past tense, after ob). [5] (hard)
severely. [6] to rebuke. [7] heathen. [8] to put. [9] Geh' und hole, go and
get (holen has the meaning of the old English "fetch"). [10] drawer. [11] to
show. [12] carefully. [13] einschlagen, schlägst, schlägt ein, schlug ein, eingeschlagen, to cover, to wrap. [14] cover. [15] to protect, to spare. [16] bringen,
brachte, gebracht, to bring (wurde, pass. voice, impf.). [17] beim Öffnen, on
opening. [18] derselben (gen. case, fem. gender), of the same, it. [19] to be
looking for, seek (as to this pres. tense in German to perf. tense in English, the following may be said : when the action or condition still con-
tinues, in German the pres. tense with the word schon, "already," or seit,
"since," is used, as : Wie lange sind Sie schon in diesem Lande? How long
have you been in this country ?).

20a. — The Spectacles Found.

A gentleman, who was engaged[1] as a city missionary[2] by[3] a
Bible-society, called upon an old lady to see if she had a Bible.
The old lady did not like[4] this gentleman's question, and
rebuked him severely with the following words: "Do you
think, sir, that I am a heathen, and have no Bible?" She then
sent[5] a girl, a young servant, who was in the room at the time,
to go and get the Bible out of the book-case[6] in another room
that she might[7] show it to the missionary. The girl brought
the Bible as she had been told.[8] The book was well preserved,[9]
and had, to all appearance,[10] been but[11] little used.[12] On
opening the Bible, the old lady exclaimed with great joy[12]:
"How very glad I am that you did come after all,[13] for here I
find my spectacles. I have been looking for them[14] these two
years,[15] and could not remember[16] where I had left[17] them[18]."

[1] anſtellen (sep. verb., reg.). [2] Stadt=Miſſionar. [3] von or bei (dat.). [4] I do not like it, es gefällt mir nicht. [5] ſchicken (reg.). [6] Bücherſchrank (m.). [7] können. [8] as she had been told = as it had been told to her, wie ihr geſagt worden war. [9] well preserved, wohl erhalten. [10] to all appearance, allem Anſcheine nach. [11] had been but little used, war nur wenig gebraucht worden. [12] Freude (f.). [13] dennoch, doch). [14] for them (sing. in German). [15] these two years, ſchon zwei Jahre, or ſeit zwei Jahren. [16] ſich erinnern, ich erinnere mich). [17] laſſen. [18] comp. 14.

---

21. Die Milch wird [1] ſauer.

Ein Mann hatte viele unglaubliche [2] Geſchichten [3] erzählt, als ein gewiſſer Profeſſor, welcher gegenwärtig [4] war, deſſen Unver= ſchämtheit [5] mit folgenden Worten abfertigte [6]: „Aber, meine Her= ren, das will nicht viel ſagen [7]; denn ich verſichere [8] Ihnen, daß der berühmte Organiſt Vogler einſt ein Gewitter [9] ſo gut darſtellte, [10] daß die Milch meilenweit [11] umher [12] ſauer wurde.“

[1] to turn. [2] incredible. [3] story. [4] present. [5] impudence. [6] to silence. [7] not amount to much. [8] to assure. [9] thunderstorm. [10] to imitate. [11] for miles. [12] around.

21a. — The Milk Turned Sour.

There are [1] a great many men, and also boys, who always [2] have a story to tell. They have a habit [3] of doing this, [4] no matter how incredible [5] these stories may be ; they seem [6] to believe them themselves. Such a man [7] was once in the company [8] of several gentlemen, to whom he told several implausible [9] stories. One of the gentlemen present, [10] who was not known [11] to the story-teller, [12] wished [13] to pay this man's impertinence in like coin, [14] and said : "But, gentlemen, it amounts to but little what this man has told. I can tell you of [15] an occurrence [16] which is better than all of his stories : I have travelled a great deal, and was present [17] once in a large city when a celebrated organist gave a concert. Among the pieces [18] which he played was one [19] in which he imitated a thunderstorm, and he did it to such perfection [20] that the milk turned sour for miles around."

[1] es giebt (indefinite idea). [2] immer. [3] Gewohnheit (f.). [4] to do this. [5] no matter how incredible, wie unglaublich auch. [6] scheinen, schien, geschienen. [7] such a man, ein solcher Mann (the indef. article must in German not only precede the noun, but also the adj. and adv., as: so good a woman, eine so gute Frau; yet in this expression, "such a man," there is a like German translation: solch ein Mann; when solch is not declined, and the meaning somewhat differs from: ein solcher Mann). [8] Gesellschaft (f.). [9] unwahrscheinlich. [10] gegenwärtig. [11] bekannt (dat.). [12] Geschichtenerzähler. [13] wünschen (reg.). [14] in like coin, in gleicher Münze. [15] von. [16] Begebenheit (f.); Vorfall (m.). [17] zugegen. [18] Stück (n.). [19] eines. [20] to such perfection, so vollkommen, or so vortrefflich.

22. Der junge Astronom.

Am Anfang[1] des siebzehnten Jahrhunderts[2] lebte in Frankreich ein berühmter Astronom, ein gewisser Gassendi, welcher ein weiser und sehr gelehrter[3] Mann war. Schon als Knabe stand[4] er oft mitten in der Nacht[5] auf,[4] um den Mond und die Sterne zu beobachten.[6] Als er sieben Jahre alt war, war er eines Abends mit mehreren[7] Spielkameraden[8] in einem Garten, und es entstand[9] ein Streit unter[10] ihnen über die Bewegung[11] des Mondes und die[12] der Wolken.[13] Die anderen Knaben, welche alle älter waren als er, behaupteten,[14] daß der Mond mit großer Schnelligkeit[15] hinter den Wolken forteile,[16] während der kleine Peter der Meinung war, daß der Mond still[17] stehe und die Wolken sich bewegten.[18] Alle Gründe,[19] die er ihnen anführte,[20] vermochten nicht,[21] sie zu überzeugen.[22] Endlich führte[23] er sie unter einen Baum, ließ sie durch die Zweige[24] nach dem Monde sehen und zeigte ihnen, wie der Mond fortwährend[25] zwischen denselben[26] Zweigen stehen blieb, während die Wolken mit großer Schnelligkeit vorüberzogen.[27]

[1] at the beginning. [2] century. [3] learned, scholarly. [4] aufstehen, stand auf, bin aufgestanden, to rise. [5] mitten in der Nacht, in the middle of the night. [6] to observe. [7] several. [8] playmate. [9] entstehen, entstand, ist entstanden, to arise. [10] among. [11] motion. [12] that of. [13] cloud. [14] to assert. [15] speed. [16] to hasten on (forteile, subj. mode after indirect

speech [oblique oration]). [17] still. [18] to move. [19] reason. [20] to adduce·
[21] could not. [22] to convince. [23] to take, to lead. [24] branch. [25] continuously. [26] the same. [27] vorüberziehen, zog vorüber, ift vorübergezogen.

22a.—The Young Astronomer.

The celebrated astronomer Gassendi, who lived at the beginning of the 17th century, gave early in his life [1] indications [2] of
great genius. [3] As a boy he would [4] rise in the middle of the
night, and look out of the window of his little room to observe
the moon and the stars. When he was about seven years old,
there arose one evening a dispute between him and his play-
mates, boys of his own [5] age, [6] concerning the motion of the
moon and the clouds. The other boys asserted that the moon
with great speed was hastening [7] on behind the clouds, while
Peter Gassendi, for that was his full name, was of the opinion
that the moon stood still and the clouds moved. When all
reasons he [8] adduced could not convince them of this fact, [9] he
took them under a tree, made them look between the branches
toward the full moon, and plainly [10] showed them how the moon
continuously stood still between the same branches while the
clouds passed on with great rapidity.

[1] früh im Leben. [2] Zeichen (n., pl. —). [3] Geift (m.), or Genie (n.).
[4] would rise, rose. [5] eigen (adj.). [6] Alter (n.). [7] was hastening, hastened. [8] Notice: a relative pronoun omitted in English must be used in
German. [9] of, von; fact, Thatfache (f.). [10] deutlich, flar.

23. Der gewiffenhafte [1] Indianer.

Ein Weißer [2] hatte eines Tages einem Indianer eine Handvoll
Tabak gegeben. Am nächften Tage kam der Indianer zu feinem
weißen Freund und gab ihm einen Viertelbollar, [3] der unter [4] dem
Tabak gewefen war, was der Weiße wahrfcheinlich [5] nicht gewußt
hatte. — Einige andere Indianer wollten ihm raten, [6] das Geld zu
behalten [7]; er aber legte die Hand auf die Bruft und fagte: „Hier

habe idj zwei Menſchen: einen guten unb einen böſen. Der gute Menſch ſagte, baß Gelb gehöre[8] nidjt mir, unb idj ſollte es bem weißen Freunb zurückbringen; ber böſe bagegen[9] behauptete,[10] baß Gelb wäre mein Eigentum; es ſei mir mit bem Tabak gegeben worben; idj könnte ganz ruhig[11] ſein unb mir Feuerwaſſer[12] bafür kaufen. Idj wußte nidjt, weſſen Rat idj folgen[13] ſollte. Um enb= lidj bie beiben Streiter[14] los[15] zu werben, ging idj zu Bett. Aber bes Streitens war kein Enbe,[16] idj mußte bas Gelb zurückbringen."

[1] conscientious. [2] a white man. [3] a quarter of a dollar. [4] among. [5] probably. [6] to advise. [7] to keep. [8] to belong (subj. mode after indirect speech). [9] on the other hand. [10] to maintain, declare, assert. [11] easy. [12] fire-water. [13] to follow, obey. [14] quarreller. [15] los werben, to get rid of. [16] no end of quarrelling.

23a. — The Conscientious Indian.

An Indian asked[1] his neighbor for[1] some tobacco. He put[2] his hand into his pocket[2] and gave him a handful. On the next morning the former came again to his neighbor, and brought[3] him back[3] a quarter of a dollar that had been among the pieces[4] of tobacco. When some one asked him why he did not keep[5] the money, he laid his hand on his heart and said: "Here in my heart I have a good and a bad man. The good man said: 'The money does not belong to you, give it back to its owner[6].' The bad man said: 'It has been given to you, it belongs to you.' The good man said to this: 'That is not true, the tobacco belongs to you, but not the money.' The bad man then said again: 'Do not be uneasy, go and buy brandy[7] with it[8].' I did not know what to do. Finally, to get rid of them, I went to bed. But the bad and the good man quarrelled[9] all night,[10] so that I had no rest[11]; I had[12] to bring back the money."

[1] to ask for, bitten um (irr. acc.). [2] to put the hand into the pocket, in bie Taſche greifen (irr.). [3] zurückbringen (sep. irr.). [4] Stück (n., pl. –e). [5] behalten (insep. irr., use subj. mode, plupf. tense). [6] Eigentümer (m.). [7] Branntwein (m.). [8] bamit, bafür. [9] ſich ſtreiten, ſtritt, geſtritten. [10] the whole night, bie ganze Nacht. [11] Ruhe (f.). [12] müſſen, mußte, gemußt.

24. Niemand fragt danach.[1]

Ein Deutscher, der bei einem Lord zu Gaste[2] war, warf[3] aus Versehen[4] ein Glas um.[3] Der Engländer war ärgerlich und fragte ihn, ob das in Deutschland Sitte (Gebrauch[5]) wäre (sei). Gefaßt[6] erwiderte der Deutsche: „Das nicht grade[7]; aber wenn es dennoch[8] geschieht, so fragt wenigstens[9] niemand danach."

[1] about it. [2] who was the guest of a lord. [3] umwerfen, wirfst, wirft um, warf um, umgeworfen = to push over, to overturn. [4] by accident. [5] custom. [6] calmly. [7] das nicht grade, not that exactly. [8] after all, however. [9] at least.

24a. — Nobody Asks about It.

A certain German gentleman, who was a great scholar,[1] and had quite[2] a high reputation[3] abroad,[4] visited England. As soon as it became known in London that this scholar had arrived,[5] he received[6] several invitations[7] from prominent[8] men there. He accepted[9] that of a certain Lord N., and at dinner had the misfortune[10] to break[11] an elegant[12] goblet. He was perfectly unconcerned[13] about the mishap,[14] but the lord, somewhat displeased,[15] as it seemed, asked him if that were customary in Germany. The German, also a little out of patience[16] at[17] this question, answered calmly: "Well, not exactly[18] a common[19] custom, yet it may happen, and if (it did), it would enter nobody's mind[20] to lose any words[21] about it."

[1] Gelehrte (decl. like an adj.). [2] ziemlich (adj.). [3] Ruf (m.). [4] im Auslande. [5] ankommen, kam an, bin angekommen. [6] erhalten, erhältst, erhält, erhielt, erhalten. [7] Einladung (f., pl. –en). [8] hervorragend, bedeutend. [9] annehmen (conj. like nehmen). [10] Unglück (n.). [11] zerbrechen, zerbrach, zerbrochen. [12] elegant, prächtig. [13] vollkommen gleichgültig. [14] Unfall (m.). [15] ungehalten. [16] außer Geduld. [17] über, bei. [18] grade. [19] gewöhnlich. [20] it would enter nobody's mind, so würde es niemandem einfallen. [21] any. words, ein Wort.

---

25. Der Böse.[1]

Ein Deutscher hatte durch den Milchhandel[2] in Philadelphia ein Vermögen[3] erworben.[4] Er ging[5] dann mit zwei Säcken[6] Gold

nach Hause und zählte[7] an Bord seinen Schatz.[8] Ein boshafter[9]
Affe auf dem Schiffe beobachtete[10] sein Vorhaben[11] und erhaschte,[12]
als der eine Sack wieder zugebunden[13] und der andere geleert[14]
war, den vollen und war bald[15] damit[16] auf der Spitze[17] des
Mastes. Hier öffnete[18] er den Sack, betrachtete[19] das schöne Gold
und warf dann ein Stück auf das Verdeck[20] und ein anderes ins
Wasser, und fuhr[21] damit fort,[21] bis er den Sack geleert hatte. Da
streckte[22] der Deutsche den Arm empor[22] und rief: „Das muß der
Böse sein; denn was vom Wasser kommt, giebt er dem Wasser
wieder, und was von der Milch kommt, giebt er mir."

[1] The evil one. [2] selling milk, milk trade. [3] fortune. [4] erwerben,
erwirbst, erwarb, erworben, (to acquire, to procure) to make. [5] (to go) to
sail. [6] Sack (m., pl. Säcke), bag. [7] to count. [8] treasure. [9] mischievous. [10] to watch. [11] doing. [12] to snatch up. [13] zubinden, band zu, zugebunden, to tie up. [14] to empty. [15] soon. [16] with it. [17] head. [18] to
open. [19] to eye. [20] deck. [21] fortfahren, fährst, fährt fort, fuhr fort, fort-
gefahren, to continue. [22] emporstrecken, to throw up.

25a. — The Evil One.

A native[1] German, who had been living in Philadelphia for
a number of years,[2] and who by selling milk had made a fortune, sold his property,[3] wishing to go home to his native country.[4] He had his money in two large bags. When he was on
board the ship, he counted over his treasure like[5] all misers.
There was a mischievous monkey on the vessel (ship) who
watched the actions of the German and, as soon as he saw an
opportunity,[7] snatched one bag and ran[8] up the main-mast[9] as
high[10] as he could. Here he imitated,[11] monkey-like,[12] what he
had seen[13] the German doing on deck, i. e. he counted the
gold. But, to the consternation[14] of the owner[15] of the gold,
he threw one piece over board[16] and one piece on deck, and
continued doing this until the bag was emptied. The German
ex-milk-merchant,[17] seeing this,[18] threw up his arms in despair[1]
and exclaimed in his native tongue[20]: "That must surely be

the evil one, for, what came from water he returns to the water, and what came from the milk he gives to me."

[1] geboren (adj.). [2] für eine Anzahl von Jahren. [3] Eigentum (n.). [4] native country, Geburtsland, Vaterland. [5] wie. [6] Geizhals (m., pl. Geizhälse). [7] Gelegenheit (f.). [8] hinaufklettern (reg.). [9] Hauptmast (m.). [10] so hoch, or so weit. [11] nachmachen (reg. dat.). [12] affenmäßig, nach Affen Weise. [13] what he had seen doing, was er hatte thun sehen. [14] zur Bestürzung. [15] Eigentümer. [16] über Bord. [17] Ex-Milchhändler. [18] when he saw this. [19] Verzweifelung (f.). [20] Muttersprache (f.).

26. Die Barbaren.[1]

Eine russische Dame war von einem Herrn zu Tische geladen,[2] und wurde durch ein unerwartetes[3] Hindernis[4] eine volle Stunde aufgehalten.[5] Die hungrigen Gäste schmollten[6] und sahen oft nach[7] ihren Uhren.[8] Als sie endlich kam, sagte einer aus der Gesellschaft[9] auf Griechisch[10] zu seinem Nachbar — weil er glaubte, sie verstehe diese Sprache nicht: — „Wenn eine Dame weder[11] jung noch[11] schön ist, so sollte sie zur rechten[12] Zeit kommen." Darauf drehte[13] sich die Dame kurz[14] herum[13] und sprach in derselben Sprache zu dem jungen Mann: „Wenn eine Dame das Unglück[15] hat, mit Barbaren zu speisen,[16] so kommt sie immer früh[17] genug."

[1] Barbarians. [2] einladen, lud ein, eingeladen, to invite (to dinner). [3] unexpected. [4] hindrance. [5] aufhalten, hältst, hält auf, hielt auf, aufgehalten. [6] to grumble. [7] at. [8] watch. [9] company. [10] in Greek. [11] weder ... noch, neither ... nor. [12] right. [13] to turn around. [14] sharply. [15] misfortune. [16] to dine (to eat). [17] soon, in time.

26a. — The Barbarians.

A gentleman and his wife[1] had been abroad, and having returned[2] to America, after an absence[3] of two years, invited their most intimate[4] friends to (dinner) dine with them, in order to see them all at the same time. The hour for dinner had arrived,[5] and all the invited[6] guests had punctually[7] presented [8] themselves, except [9] a lady, who, to her great regret,[10] had been detained by an unexpected hindrance. The host,[11] hostess [11] and guests waited [12] a quarter of an hour,[13] half an hour and, with some signs [14] of impatience,[15] three-quarters of an hour,[16] and when she finally arrived, a full hour had passed [17] beyond [18] the appointed [19] time. The lady was known to but [20] few [21] of the guests, she being [22] a new acquaintance [23] of the lady and gentleman of the house. There were present two young gentlemen, also strangers [24] to the lady, and one of them, who had especially [25] shown signs of impatience at [26] the delayed [27] dinner, wishing to express [28] his feelings,[29] remarked to his friend in Greek, thinking [30] the lady would not understand this language : " If a lady is neither young nor beautiful, she should come in time." The lady, however, turned sharply to the speaker,[31] and replied in the same language : " When a lady has the misfortune to be in the company of barbarians, she always comes in time [32]."

[1] Gemahlin (f.). [2] zurückkehren (reg. comp. sep. verb). [3] Abwesenheit (f.). [4] vertraut, intim. [5] herankommen (comp. sep. verb; irr. like kommen; aux. "to be," sein). [6] eingeladen (adj.). [7] pünktlich (adv.). [8] to present themselves, sich einstellen (comp. sep. verb, reg.). [9] außer (prep., dat.). [10] zu ihrem großen Bedauern. [11] Herr und Dame des Hauses. [12] warten (reg.). [13] eine Viertelstunde. [14] some signs = Zeichen. [15] von Ungeduld. [16] drei Viertelstunden. [17] vergehen, verging, ist vergangen. [18] über. [19] bestimmt (adj.). [20] and [21] known to but few, nur wenigen bekannt. [22] she was. [23] Bekannte (f.). [24] also strangers to the lady, der Dame auch fremd. [25] besonders. [26] über. [27] verspätet (adj.). [28] ausdrücken (reg.). [29] Gefühl (n.). [30] as he thought. [31] to him, who had spoken. [32] zur rechten Zeit.

27. Drei Kronen.[1]

Karoline, die Königin von England, dachte eines Tages daran,[2] den königlichen Palast und seine Umgebungen [3] zu verbessern;[4] unter anderem [5] den öffentlichen [6] St. James Park zu schließen [7] und ihn in einen Garten für den Hof umzuschaffen.[8] Sie fragte daher ihren Premierminister,[9] Walpole, was das kosten würde. Der Minister antwortete schnell: „Drei Kronen."

[1] Crown: the emblem of royalty and also an English silver coin of the value of five shillings. A double meaning is here intended. [2] dachte daran, thought of (improving). [3] surroundings. [4] to improve. [5] among other things. [6] public. [7] ſchließen, ſchloß, geſchloſſen, to close. [8] umſchaffen, ſchuf um, umgeſchaffen, to transform, to change. [9] Prime-minister.

27a. — Three Crowns.

It once occurred[1] to Caroline, Queen of England, to have[2] the surroundings of the royal palace in London improved.[3] She wished among other things to close St. James Park, at the time a public place, and to convert it into a royal garden. She therefore asked her prime-minister, Robert Walpole, how much this change[3] would cost. Robert Walpole, quick-witted,[4] and with a striking[5] answer at hand,[6] replied: "Three crowns, your majesty." — It is easily to be seen that this answer contained a double meaning; but the queen very likely chose[7] the one[8] intended for her, and also followed[9] the good advice that lay[10] in this answer.

[1] einfallen, fällſt, fällt ein, fiel ein, iſt eingefallen; es fällt mir ein, it occurs to me. [2] to have ... improved, verbeſſern laſſen. [3] Veränderung. (f.). [4] ſcharfſinnig, von raſchem Witz. [5] ſchlagend (adj.). [6] bei der Hand. [7] wählen (reg.). [8] that which was intended for her, die, welche für ſie beſtimmt war. [9] folgen (reg., dat.). [10] liegen, lag, iſt gelegen.

---

28. Einer zur Zeit.

Als Heinrich der Vierte durch eine kleine Stadt kam, bemerkte[1] er, daß ſich die Einwohner[2] verſammelten,[3] um ihn bei ſeiner Ankunft[4] zu bewillkommnen.[5] Gerade als der Bürgermeiſter[6] in der Mitte einer langweiligen[7] Rede[8] war, fing[9] ein Eſel an[9] zu ſchreien.[10] Darauf wandte ſich der König gegen[11] den Ort, wo das Tier ſtand, und ſagte: „Meine Herren, einer zur Zeit, wenn es gefällig iſt[12]."

[1] to notice, to perceive. [2] inhabitants. [3] to assemble. [4] arrival. [5] to congratulate. [6] mayor. [7] tedious. [8] speech, oration. [9] anfangen, fing an, angefangen, to begin. [10] to bray. [11] towards. [12] if you please.

28a. — One at a Time.

Henry IV., king of England, was once on a journey through the country. When he approached [1] a small city, he noticed that the citizens, [2] who had heard of his coming, had assembled to receive him with honor. The mayor, the first man of the city, made a rather [3] long and tedious speech full of [4] flattering phrases, [5] etc. When he was about the middle of his oration, an ass near by [7] began to bray. The king then turned towards the place from which the noise [8] came, and made the following witty remark [9]: "Not all at once, [10] gentlemen; one at a time, if you please."

[1] ſich nähern (reg., dat.). [2] Bürger (m., pl. —). [3] ziemlich (adv.). [4] voll von. [5] ſchmeichelhaft (adj.). [6] Phraſe (f.), Redensart (f., pl. -en). [7] nahe bei, in der Nähe. [8] Lärm (m.). [9] Bemerkung (f.). [10] auf einmal.

29. Engliſcher Nebel.[1]

Der engliſche Nebel war zu allen Zeiten die Klage [2] der Fremden. Ein Freund Gondomars, des ſpaniſchen Geſandten, [3] machte dieſem ſeine Aufwartung [4] und fragte: „Haben Sie etwas nach Spanien zu beſtellen [5]?" Gondomar antwortete: „Nur meine Empfehlung [6] an [7] die Sonne, welche ich nicht geſehen habe, ſeit ich in England bin [8]."

[1] fog. [2] complaint. [3] ambassador. [4] Aufwartung machen, to wait on, to pay a visit. [5] any orders, any commands. [6] compliments. [7] to. [8] have been.

29a. — English Fog.

The fogs of England, and especially of London, are [1] spoken [2] of in all parts of the world. They have become proverbial, [3] and strangers living [4] in London have at all times complained [5] of them. One day a Spaniard, shortly [6] before his departure [7] from London, paid a visit to the Spanish ambassador, and when taking [8] leave, asked him if he had any message [9] to Spain. The ambassador, whose name was Gondomar, replied: "Noth-

ing, sir, nothing to [10] my government, only my compliments to
the sun, which I have not seen these [11] six months that I have
been in England."

[1] passive voice. [2] befprochen (comp. insep. irr. verb, like fprechen, to
speak). [3] fprichwörtlich. [4] who live. [5] fich beflagen über. [6] furz.
[7] Abreife (f., pl. –en). [8] when he took leave (Abfchied). [9] Senbung (f., pl.
–en). Botfchaft (f., pl. –en). [10] an (acc.). [11] feit ben fechs Monaten.

30. Den Geist aufgeben.[1]

Ein Schaufpieler fpielte ben Geift in „Hamlet" fehr fchlecht[2] unb
wurbe ausgezifcht.[3] Nachbem[4] er biefes eine Zeit lang[5] ertragen[6]
hatte, verfetzte[7] er bie Zufchauer[8] baburch[9] in gute Laune,[10] baß[9]
er vortrat[11] unb fagte: „Meine Damen unb Herren, es thut[12] mir
außerorbentlich[13] leib,[12] baß meine Bemühungen,[14] Ihnen zu gefal=
len, erfolglos[15] finb, wenn Sie aber nicht zufrieden[16] finb, fo muß
ich ben Geift aufgeben."

[1] to give up. [2] badly. [3] to hiss. [4] after. [5] for a time. [6] ertragen,
erträgft, erträgt, ertrug, ertragen, to bear, to endure, to suffer. [7] to put.
[8] audience. [9] baburch, baß = by (followed by pres. part.). [10] humor.
[11] vortreten, trittft, tritt vor, trat vor, vorgetreten, fein = to step forward.
[12] leib thun, es thut mir leib, I am sorry. [13] extremely. [14] endeavor.
[15] unsuccessful. [16] satisfied.

30a. — Giving up the Ghost.

When an actor has the misfortune to displease[1] the audience,
he may, perchance,[2] save[3] his good reputation by[4] making a
joke[5] right on the spot.[6] The hero of our anecdote is an actor,
who seems to have played the Ghost in " Hamlet " very poorly,
and was hissed. He bore this for a time, until[7] it occurred to
him that he must[8] do something to turn[9] the humor of the
audience in his favor.[10] He succeeded[11] in his plan[12] by step-
ping to the front[13] and saying : " Ladies and gentlemen, my
efforts to please you seem to be wholly[14] unsuccessful, and I am
exceedingly sorry ; but, if I cannot satisfy[15] you, it will be best[16]
for me to give up the ghost."

¹ mißfallen (comp. insep. verb, irr., like fallen, dat.).　² vielleicht.
³ retten (reg.).　⁴ thereby, that he, dadurch, daß.　⁵ Scherz (m.), Witz (m.).
⁶ right on the spot, gleich auf der Stelle = sogleich.　⁷ bis (subord. conj.).
⁸ müsse (subj. mode, pres. tense, in indirect speech).　⁹ wenden.　¹⁰ in his
favor, zu seinen Gunsten.　¹¹ gelingen, gelang, ist gelungen (impersonal
verb, es gelingt mir).　¹² mit seinem Plan.　¹³ to step to the front, vortre=
ten.　¹⁴ gänzlich.　¹⁵ zufrieden stellen.　¹⁶ am besten.

31. Weisheit.¹

Als man² Thales fragte,² was das schwierigste³ und was das
leichteste Ding in der Welt wäre,⁴ antwortete er: „Das schwierigste
ist, sich selbst kennen⁵ zu lernen,⁶ und das leichteste, an⁷ den Hand=
lungen⁸ Anderer Tadel⁷ zu finden."

¹ Wisdom.　² man fragte, was asked (passive).　³ difficult.　⁴ wäre
(subj. mode after indirect question).　⁵ sich, etc. = to know one's self.
⁶ to learn.　⁷ Tadel finden an, to find fault with.　⁸ actions.

31a. — Wisdom.

Thales, one of the wise men¹ of Greece,² on being³ asked
one day by⁴ one of his scholars, what was the most difficult
and what the easiest thing in the world, answered: "The most
difficult thing in the world is to know one's self, and the easiest
to find fault with the actions of others."

[What a wise saying!⁵ Would that all people might⁶ take it
to heart.⁷ But, alas, our experience⁸ of to-day⁹ is, that the
world takes the easiest. Most people know their neighbors'
affairs¹⁰ better than their own.¹¹ A German proverb says:
"Sweep first before your own door¹²."]

¹ wise man, der Weise (decl. like an adj.).　² Griechenland (n.).　³ when
he was asked (passive).　⁴ von.　⁵ what, etc. = welch ein weiser Spruch!
⁶ daß doch ... möchten.　⁷ to take to heart, zu Herzen nehmen.　⁸ Erfahrung
(f.).　⁹ of to-day, heutigen Tages.　¹⁰ Angelegenheit (f., pl. —en).　¹¹ ihre
eigenen.　¹² „Kehre erst vor deiner Thür."

32. An die Laterne.[1]

Ein französischer Abt,[2] welcher sich während der französischen
Revolution bei[3] den Demokraten verhaßt[4] gemacht hatte, wurde in
einer Nacht vom Pöbel[5] ergriffen[6] und nach einer Laterne ge=
schleppt.[7] „Bitte,[8] Freunde,“ sagte der Abt, „glaubt ihr, daß ihr
besser sehen könnt, wenn ihr mich an die Laterne hängt?“ Dieser
Witz beruhigte[9] das Gesindel[10] und rettete dem Abt das Leben.

[1] Lamp-post. [2] abbot, abbé. [3] to. [4] obnoxious. [5] mob. [6] ergrei-
fen, ergriff, ergriffen, to seize. [7] to drag. [8] pray. [9] to pacify. [10] rabble.

32a. — To the Lamp-Post.

A French abbé who, during the Revolution in France, had
made himself obnoxious to the stronger[1] party,[2] the democrats,
was seized one night by the mob, as many a one before and
after him[3] has been, and dragged to a lamp-post. This would
not have been, under ordinary[4] circumstances,[5] a very serious[6]
matter[7]; but it meant[8] death in those days. The abbé, however, was resolved[9] not to be outwitted,[10] even[11] at[12] the most
critical[13] moment.[14] He said to the mob : “Citizens, do you
think you can see any better, if you hang me to that lamp-
post?” This witticism had the desired[15] effect[16]; it appeased
the rabble, and saved the abbé's life.

[1] stark, stärker, stärkst. [2] Partei (f.). [3] wie viele (mancher) vor und nach
ihm. [4] gewöhnlich. [5] Umstand (m., pl. Umstände). [6] serious, wichtig, ge-
fährlich. [7] Sache (f.). [8] bedeuten (reg.). [9] entschlossen. [10] überlisten (reg.,
passive voice). [11] sogar. [12] im. [13] kritisch, entscheidend, bedenklich. [14] Au-
genblick (m.). [15] erwünscht. [16] Erfolg (m.).

33. In der[1] Tasche.

Als der Graf[2] von Grancé von einer Flintenkugel[3] im Knie
verwundet[4] war, machten die Wundärzte[5] mehrere Einschnitte.[6]
Zuletzt verlor der Graf die Geduld und fragte, warum sie ihn so

unbarmherzig behandelten[7]: „Wir suchen die Kugel," sagten sie. „Teufel! warum sagtet ihr das nicht vorher?" erwiderte der Graf, „ich habe sie in der Tasche."

[1] my. [2] count. [3] musket-ball. [4] to wound. [5] surgeons. [6] incisions.
[7] cruelly treated.

33a. — In my Pocket.

The Count of Grancé was a French officer, and was well-known in military[1] circles.[2] It came to pass[3] one day in a battle, that he was wounded in his knee by a musket-ball. The surgeons were[4] at once called, and they went to[5] work with lancet[6] and probe[7] to search[8] for the ball. In those days chloroform[9] and ether[10] were not known to the medical[11] profession,[12] and in operations[13] of this kind[14] the pain[15] had[16] to be patiently endured.[17] The surgeons had, for a considerable[18] time, caused[19] the general a great deal of pain, when he at last[20] lost his patience, and asked them, if it was necessary to treat him so unmercifully, and what they were[21] doing with his knee for so long a[22] time. The surgeons, astonished[23] at this question, said that they were looking for the ball. Upon this[24] the count was almost[25] beside himself, and cried[26] with[27] rage[28]: "Thunder[29]! why did you not ask me before,[30] you quacks[31]? I have the bullet in my right vest-pocket."

[1] militärisch. [2] Kreis (m., pl. —e). [3] it came to pass, it happened. [4] Passive voice. [5] to go to work, sich an die Arbeit machen. [6] Lanzette (f.). [7] Sonde (f.). [8] to search for, suchen (reg.). [9] Chloroform (n.). [10] Äther (m.). [11] medizinisch. [12] Stand (m.). [13] Operation (f., pl. —en), bei Operationen. [14] dieser Art. [15] Schmerz (m., pl. —en). [16] müssen, mußte, gemußt. [17] ertragen (comp. insep. verb, irr., like tragen; "to be endured," passive voice). [18] ziemlich lange. [19] verursachen (reg., dat.). [20] zuletzt. [21] the subj. mode after indirect question. [22] for a so long time. [23] astonished at, erstaunt über (acc.). [24] darauf. [25] beinahe; almost beside himself, beinahe außer sich. [26] rufen, rief, gerufen. [27] vor. [28] Wut (f.), Ärger (m.), Zorn (m.). [29] Donnerwetter! Zum Teufel! [30] vorher. [31] Quacksalber.

It may reasonably be expected, after this, that the pupils will be able to work more independently. For this reason it seems no longer necessary to have the original German text precede the English anecdote. The notes also will be found to be less copious, as it is now desirable that the pupil should become more familiar with the lexicon. Neither will the parts of the irregular verbs be given any longer; indications, however, will be found for a time as to whether the verbs are separable, inseparable or irregular.

PART SECOND.

1. Planting Trees.[1]

A very poor (and) old man had only a little hut,[2] around[3] which (there) was a small piece[4] of land. In one part of this land he had planted vegetables[5] and flowers. One day he was digging[6] with a spade[7] in the other part. A man, much younger than he, who was passing[8] that way, stopped and asked him what he was doing.[9] The old man looked up,[10] leaned[11] on his spade and answered: " I am planting trees." "Trees !" replied the younger man, "you certainly cannot expect[12] to eat the fruit of them." "I cannot and do not expect to eat the fruit of these trees; but I have during all[13] my life eaten fruit, and I like it now. Someone planted trees before[14] I was born,[15] and I have eaten the fruit thereof.[16] I now am planting trees that others may eat the fruit, and that a sign of my gratitude[17] may be left[18] when I am gone[19]."

[1] Bäume pflanzen. [2] Hütte (f.). [3] um (prep. acc.). [4] Stück (n.). [5] Gemüse (n., pl. —). [6] graben (irr.). [7] Spaten (m.). [8] to pass that way, da or dort vorbeigehen (sep., irr.). [9] Subj. mode after indirect question. [10] auffehen (sep., irr.). [11] lehnen (reg.). [12] erwarten (reg.). [13] all, ganz (when the English word "all" has the meaning of "whole," the German is ganz). [14] ehe (sub. conj.). [15] geboren. [16] davon. [17] Dankbarkeit (f.). [18] may be left, mag zurückbleiben. [19] sterben (aux. fein; when I have died, wenn ich gestorben bin).

2. His Head when he was a Boy.

Two strangers once went to[1] a museum in London. They had a guide,[2] who showed them everything[3] that was remarkable.[4] Among many other things he showed a skull,[5] and told them it was that of Oliver Cromwell. Now, as this skull was quite small, one of the strangers said: "How could so great a man have so small a head?" "Ah, well⁶!" said the guide, "that was his head when he was a boy."

¹ in ... Mufe′um. ² Führer. ³ alles, was. ⁴ merkwürdig. ⁵ Schä-del (m.). ⁶ Ja, nun!

———

Beantworten Sie auf beutsch bie folgenden Fragen:

Wie viele Fremde haben wir hier, unb wohin gingen sie?

Wer war bei ihnen, unb was sahen sie unter vielen Merkwürdig= keiten (curiosities)?

Da biefer Schädel sehr klein war, was sagte einer der Fremden?

War biefer Schädel groß genug für ben eines Mannes?

———

3. The Donkey laden¹ with Sponges.²

A donkey that was laden with two bags wanted to wade³ through a brook⁴; but he slipped⁵ on the loose⁶ stones and fell into the water. When he stood up again, he felt⁷ that his load had become⁸ much lighter, for he was laden with salt,⁹ and a large part of it had melted.¹⁰ This occurrence¹¹ the donkey bore in mind.¹² When he came back again with a heavy load, and was again in the water, he did not fall this time,¹³ but lay down purposely.¹⁴ But, oh, misfortune! he could not get¹⁵ up again this time; his burden¹⁶ had become much heavier. He was laden with sponges, which filled¹⁷ at once¹⁸ with water, and became so heavy that he lost his life.

¹ belaben. ² Schwamm (m., pl. Schwämme). ³ waten (reg.). ⁴ Bach (m.). ⁵ schlüpfen (reg.). ⁶ los. ⁷ fühlen (reg.). ⁸ werden (irr.). ⁹ Salz (n.). ¹⁰ schmelzen (irr. sein). ¹¹ Vorfall (m.). ¹² to bear in mind, sich merken (reg.). ¹³ biefes Mal. ¹⁴ absichtlich. ¹⁵ aufstehen (sep. irr.). ¹⁶ Last (f.), Labung (f.). ¹⁷ sich füllen (reg.). ¹⁸ sogleich.

———

4. Sir Isaac Newton's Dinner.

Sir Isaac Newton had invited a friend to dinner, and forgot¹ to tell his housekeeper² anything³ about it.⁴ The next day⁵ his friend came at noon,[6] and found Newton in deep thought, as (it) was usual with[7] him.   Dinner[8] was served,[9] but, of course, only for one.   The friend, without disturbing Newton, sat down and helped[10] himself.   When the philosopher had recovered[11] from his reveries,[12] he looked at the empty dishes[13] and said: "Well, really,[14] if the proof[15] were not before my eyes, i. e. if I did[16] not see the empty dishes and plates,[17] I should[18] say I had not yet dined[19]."

[1] vergeſſen (irr.).   [2] Haushälterin (f.).   [3] etwas.   [4] davon.   [5] Acc. definite time.   [6] um Mittag.   [7] bei.   [8] Definite article.   [9] auftragen (sep., irr., passive voice).   [10] zulangen (regular), bedienen (reg.).   [11] ſich erholen (reg.).   [12] Träumerei (f., pl. -en).   [13] Schlüſſel (f., pl. —).   [14] wirklich.   [15] Beweis (m.).   [16] Subj. mode, impf. tense, after wenn, conditionally.   [17] Teller (m., pl. —).   [18] I should say, ich würde ſagen, ich ſollte denken, ich ſollte meinen.   [19] zu Mittag ſpeiſen.

---

4. Pulling[1] the wrong[2] Tooth.[3]

A man named[4] Snow was going along the street[5] and held his handkerchief[6] to[7] his cheek.[8]   He met one of his acquaintances,[9] who stopped, spoke to[10] him, and asked him what was the matter with his face.[11]   Mr. Snow told his friend that he had[12] had the toothache,[13] and that his cheek was swollen.[14] "Why, that is nothing," said the other, "go to[15] a dentist[16] and have[17] it drawn."   "Well, I have just been to[18] a dentist," replied the former, "to have my tooth drawn, but he made a mistake."   "How a mistake?" asked the latter.   "He drew the wrong tooth, and I was angry enough, I can assure[19] you." "And what did he say then?"   "Well, that is all settled[20]; he did not[21] charge[22] anything[21] for it," was the answer.   "I knew[8] it would end[23] that way.[24]   You are always in luck[25]."

[1] ausziehen (sep., irr.).   [2] unrecht, falſch.   [3] Zahn (m., pl. Zähne).   [4] Namens.   [5] die Straße entlang.   [6] Taſchentuch (n., pl. -tücher).   [7] an (acc.).   [8] Backe (f.), Wange (f.).   [9] Bekannte (m., decl. like an adj.).   [10] mit.   [11] what was . . . face, was mit ſeinem Geſichte los wäre (subj. mode after indirect question).   [12] Subj. mode after indirect speech.   [13] Zahnweh (n.),

Zahnschmerzen (pl.). ¹⁴ geschwollen (past part. of schwellen). ¹⁵ zu (dat.). ¹⁶ Zahnarzt (m.). ¹⁷ have it, cause it to be = lassen (with infin.). ¹⁸ bei (dat.). ¹⁹ versichern (reg. acc.). ²⁰ abgemacht, in Ordnung. ²¹ not anything, nichts. ²² fordern. ²³ enden (reg.). ²⁴ auf diese Weise. ²⁵ you are in luck = you have luck.

5. Living¹ on Air.

A gentleman once told a lady that an apothecary,² a friend of hers,³ had become bankrupt.⁴ When she asked him "why," he told her that her friend was a very honest⁵ man, and had advised⁶ his patients⁷ to breathe⁸ pure⁹ air instead¹⁰ of taking medicine.¹¹ People then followed¹² his advice. He could not sell¹³ his goods,¹⁴ and was obliged¹⁵ to give¹⁶ up business. "Poor man!" she replied, "what a pity¹⁷ he could not live on air, as he had advised his patients (to do)."

¹ to live on, leben von. ² Apothe′ker (m.). ³ of hers, von ihr. ⁴ to become bankrupt, Bankerott machen (subj. mode, indirect speech). ⁵ aufrichtig, ehrlich, rechtschaffen. ⁶ raten (irr., dat.). ⁷ Patient (m., pl. -en). ⁸ atmen (reg.). ⁹ rein, frisch. ¹⁰ instead to take. ¹¹ Medizin (f.). ¹² folgen (reg., dat.). ¹³ verkaufen (reg.). ¹⁴ Ware (f., pl. -en). ¹⁵ to be obliged, müssen. ¹⁶ aufgeben (sep.). ¹⁷ what a pity, wie schade.

Beantworten Sie auf deutsch die folgenden Fragen:

Wem erzählte ein Herr, daß ein Apotheker Bankerott gemacht hätte?

Kannte diese Dame diesen Apotheker?

Was hatte der Apotheker seinen Patienten geraten?

Was war die Folge (consequence) dieses Rates?

Was halten Sie (think of) von einem solchen Geschäftsmann?

6. Simplicity.¹

A gentleman, who had a very simple² servant, wished to rise very early one morning. Therefore he told his servant the previous³ evening to call him at⁴ five the next morning.⁵ In

the morning the servant was in his master's room at four; but
his master being still asleep, he did not awake[6] him.   As soon
as his master awoke[7]— it was seven o'clock — he asked John
what time[8] it was.   When he heard the time, he said : "Why
did you not come at five?"   "Sir," answered John, "I was
here at four, but you were asleep, and I dared[9] not disturb[10]
you."

[1] Einfalt (f.).   [2] einfältig.   [3] vorher (adverb).   [4] um.   [5] Acc. of
definite time.   [6] wecken (reg.).   [7] erwachen (reg.).   [8] wie viel Uhr (followed
by subj. after an indirect question).   [9] to dare, to venture, to risk, wagen
(reg.).   [10] stören (reg.).

_____

Beantworten Sie auf deutsch die folgenden Fragen :

Was für einen Diener hatte ein Herr?

Wie hieß dieser Diener?

Um wie viel Uhr wollte der Herr den folgenden Morgen auf=
stehen?

War der Diener früh genug im Zimmer, um seinen Herrn zur
rechten Zeit zu wecken?

Warum weckte er aber seinen Herrn nicht?

Wie viele Stunden (hours) später stand der Herr auf, als er
wünschte?

_____

7. Good Glass.

About forty years ago,[1] when a certain Rev. D. D.[2] was pastor[2]
of a church[3] in the state[4] of Massachusetts, he once conducted[5]
an evening-service.[6]   This service was in a little wooden[7]
chapel[8] that stood by the side of[9] the church.   The pulpit[10] was
very plain,[11] and was lighted[12] by[13] two small oil-lamps.[14]   As
the reverend gentleman was offering prayer,[15] he made a
gesture,[16] and pushed[17] one of the lamps in front of him[18] upon
the floor.[19]   He quickly[20] opened his eyes, and looked down.[21]
Seeing that the lamp was not broken,[22] he remarked : "Well, it
was good glass anyway[23]."   He then closed his eyes again, and
went on[24] with[25] his prayer where he had left off.[26]

[1] ago = before, vor (dat.; this prep. must always precede the object; it may precede or follow the adverb, as: ungefähr vor vierzig Jahren, vor ungefähr v. J.). [2] Ehrwürden D. D. (*Divinitatis Doctor*); Pastor, Pfarrer, Prediger. [3] Kirche (f.). [4] Staat (m.). [5] leiten (reg.). [6] Abend-Gottesdienst (m.). [7] hölzern. [8] Kapelle (f.). [9] by the side of, beside, neben (dat. after a verb of rest). [10] Kanzel (f.). [11] einfach. [12] erleuchten (reg., passive). [13] von (dat.), or durch (acc.). [14] Öllampe (f., pl. -n). [15] to offer prayer, to pray, beten (reg.). [16] eine Bewegung mit der Hand. [17] stoßen (irr.). [18] in front of him, before him. [19] Boden (m.). [20] schnell. [21] to look down, hinunterblicken (sep., reg.). [22] zerbrechen (insep., irr.). [23] auf jeden Fall, jedenfalls. [24] to go on, to continue, fortfahren (sep., irr.). [25] in, or mit (dat.). [26] to leave off, aufhören, sep., reg., or stehen bleiben; (sein).

---

8. The Quaker[1] and Benjamin Franklin.

There once lived in Philadelphia a Quaker who was very rich, and who had a large collection[2] of rare[3] books. When Benjamin Franklin lived there, he became acquainted[4] with this Quaker, and was[5] often invited by him to come and see[6] him. It was the library[7] especially that gave[8] Franklin great pleasure. One day, shortly before Franklin's departure[9] to England, he was again at[10] his friend's house, and as he was on the point[11] of taking his leave,[12] the Quaker showed him a shorter way to[13] the street through a rather[14] dark passage.[15] When Franklin was in this passage the Quaker called[16] after him: "Stoop![17] stoop!" Franklin did not comprehend[18] then what he meant, and went along.[19] Suddenly[20] he ran[21] his head so violently[22] against[23] a cross-beam,[24] which he had not noticed in the dark, that he almost fell to[25] the ground. Not until then[26] did Franklin understand fully[27] the Quaker's warning[28] words.

[1] Quäker. (m.). [2] Sammlung (f., pl. -en). [3] selten, or rar. [4] bekannt. [5] Passive voice. [6] to come to see, besuchen (reg.). [7] Bibliothek (f.). [8] machen (reg.); to give great pleasure, großes Vergnügen machen, or verschaffen. [9] Abreise (f.). [10] bei seinem Freund. [11] to be on the point of, im Begriff sein ... zu. [12] to take leave, Abschied nehmen (irr.). [13] nach (dat.), or auf (acc.). [14] ziemlich (adv.). [15] Durchgang (m.). [16] nachrufen (sep., irr., dat.). [17] sich bücken (reg.). [18] begreifen (reg.). [19] dahin-

gehen (sep., irr.), or feines Weges gehen. ²⁰ plötzlich. ²¹ ftoßen (irr.).
²² heftig, ftart. ²³ gegen (acc.). ²⁴ Querbalfen (m.). ²⁵ auf. ²⁶ not until
then, dann erft, or erft dann. ²⁷ völlig, vollftändig. ²⁸ warnend (adj.).

---

9. The poor Comedian.¹

A poor comedian, who had wit enough, but little money to
pay for his dinner, went one day to visit² a banker, known for³
his riches,⁴ as well as for his avarice,⁵ and proposed⁶ to him a
transaction,⁷ in which there were, as he said, a hundred thousand dollars to be gained.⁸ As it was just at dinner-time,⁹ and
the banker was about to sit down at the table,¹⁰ he invited the
comedian to dine with him. The latter accepted.¹¹ After
dinner the banker asked the caller¹² some particulars¹³ regard-
ing¹⁴ the operation¹⁵ of which he had spoken. "Sir," said the
comedian, "I have been told¹⁶ that you will give two hundred
thousand dollars as a dowry¹⁷ to your daughter. Well, I will
take her for half¹⁸ that sum. It is clear that, in granting¹⁹ me
the hand of your daughter, you will gain a hundred thousand
dollars."

¹ Schaufpieler (m.), Komödiant (m.). ² to visit a b.=zu einem Bankier.
³ wegen (gen.). ⁴ Reichtum (m.). ⁵ Geiz (m.). ⁶ vorfchlagen (sep., irr.).
⁷ Gefchäft (n.), or Unternehmen (n.). ⁸ to be gained, zu gewinnen (in German the active voice follows "to be." ⁹ Mittagszeit (f.). ¹⁰ to sit down
at the table, fich zu Tifche fetzen. ¹¹ accepted it, es annehmen (sep., irr.).
¹² Befucher (m.). ¹³ einige Punkte, Einzelheiten. ¹⁴ in Bezug auf (acc.).
¹⁵ See note 7. ¹⁶ I have been told, es ift mir gefagt worden, man hat mir
gefagt. ¹⁷ Mitgift (f.). ¹⁸ for half that sum, für die Hälfte diefer Summe,
or für die halbe Summe. ¹⁹ to grant, bewilligen (reg., in granting = when
you grant).

---

10. Frederick II. and the Deserter.¹

Frederick II. (the second), king of Prussia, also called the
Great, or the only One,² or, by the Empress of Austria, "The
Bad Man," was a great as well as a good soldier, and many
interesting³ stories are told⁴ of him. He was liked by his
soldiers no less⁵ than he was feared by his enemies. It was at

the time of the Seven Years'[6] War, a battle was expected[7] on
the following day, and, well[8] knowing that the enemy outnum-
bered him[9] three to one,[10] he and every soldier feared that the
battle would not turn[11] out fortunately for him. He, therefore,
on the evening before, was rather restless[12] in his tent,[13] and
went out[14] to make a nocturnal round[15] through his camp[16] to
see if his soldiers were in any way[17] disheartened.[18] On this
round he soon saw a soldier who was trying[19] to avoid[20] him,
and who acted[21] in[22] a suspicious[23] and mysterious[24] manner.[25]
The king knew at once that all was not right[26] — for no honest
soldier was ever[27] afraid of[28] his king, — and so he challenged[29]
him. The soldier saw no possibility[30] of escaping,[31] so he
stopped, and stood before the king, saluting[32] him in military
style.[33] Upon the question: "Where were you going?" the
soldier answered with embarrassment,[34] but frankly[35] : "To con-
fess[36] openly,[37] your Majesty, I was on the point of deserting[38]."
The king, instead of calling the guard[39] to have this disloyal[40]
soldier arrested,[41] said to him in good humor: "It is true,
friend, our prospects[42] for to-morrow are not of[43] the best ; but
try it with me once more,[44] and if the battle to-morrow does
not turn out in our favor,[45] we will desert together." The soldier needed[46] no further[47] urging[48] ; his king had been kind to
him, he loved His Majesty, and he gladly[49] staid,[50] helping[51] to
win the battle on the next day over[52] the Austrian[53] army, and
neither he nor the king found it necessary to desert.

---

[1] Überläufer (m.). [2] der Einzige. [3] interessant, unterhaltend. [4] are told
(pass. voice). [5] nicht weniger. [6] siebenjährig (adj.). [7] erwarten (reg.).
[8] da er wohl wußte. [9] übertraf ihn an Zahl. [10] drei gegen einen. [11] to
turn out, ausfallen (sep., irr.). [12] unruhig. [13] Zelt (n.). [14] hinausgehen
(sep., irr.). [15] nocturnal round, eine nächtliche Runde. [16] Lager (n.).
[17] irgendwie. [18] entmutigt. [19] versuchen (reg.). [20] vermeiden (reg.), or ihm
aus dem Wege zu gehen. [21] handeln (reg.), or sich benehmen (irr.). [22] auf
(acc.). [23] verdächtig. [24] geheim. [25] Weise (f.). [26] all is not right, nicht
alles ist richtig. [27] je. [28] to be afraid of, sich fürchten vor (dat.). [29] anrufen
(sep., irr.). [30] Möglichkeit (f., pl. -en). [31] entkommen (insep., irr.), or
entfliehen (insep., irr.). [32] saluting = and saluted, salutieren, grüßen (reg.).

[33] Art (f.), Weiſe (f.). [34] Verlegenheit (f., pl. –en), or Verwirrung (f., pl. –en). [35] franf, frei, offenherzig. [36] geſtehen. [37] offen. [38] deſertieren. [39] Wache (f., pl. –en). [40] treulos. [41] arretieren, verhaften. [42] Ausſicht (f., pl. –en). [43] of the best, zum Beſten. [44] once more, noch einmal. [45] does not turn out in our favor, nicht zu unſeren Gunſten ausfällt, or von gutem Erfolg für uns. [46] brauchen (reg.). [47] weiter, ferner (adj.). [48] Antreiben, Zureden (n.). [49] gern, mit Freuden. [50] bleiben (irr.). [51] helping, helfen (irr.); helping to win, gewinnen helfen. [52] über (acc.). [53] öſterreichiſch.

---

11. Misunderstanding [1] of Henry VIII. with Francis I., King of France.

Henry VIII., king of England, once had a misunderstanding with Francis I., king of France, and concluded [2] to send [3] a minister to France with the order, [4] to call the French king to account [5] with harsh, [6] severe [7] words. But the minister, considering [8] the message [9] too severe, thought his life would be in danger, and said to his king: "Your Majesty, Francis I., is a proud, quick-tempered monarch, and if I deliver [11] your message in these insulting [12] words, he will surely [13] have me beheaded. [14] The king then said to him: "Fear nothing! Should the French king have you beheaded, I shall take [15] off the head of every Frenchman whom I have in my power [16] in England." "I readily [17] believe your Majesty," replied the minister, "but what I do not believe is, that there is one among all those French heads which will [18] fit [19] upon my shoulders [20] as well as the one that sits upon them now."

[1] Mißverſtändnis (n., pl. –ſſe). [2] beſchließen (insep., irr., like ſchließen). [3] ſenden, ſandte, geſandt. [4] Auftrag (m., pl. Aufträge). [5] to call to account, zur Rechenſchaft ziehen. [6] barſch. [7] ſtreng, heftig. [8] to consider, halten für. [9] Botſchaft (f., pl. –en). [10] hitzig. [11] überliefern (insep., reg.). [12] beleidigend. [13] ſicherlich. [14] enthaupten (insep., reg.). [15] to take off, abhauen (sep., irr.), abſchlagen (sep., irr.). [16] Gewalt (f.). [17] gern. [18] Future or present tense. [19] paſſen. [20] Schulter (f.).

---

12. The Law [1] of Retaliation. [2]

A slater, [3] who was one day working [4] high [5] upon a roof, [6] slipped, [7] and fell upon the street. It so happened that he fell on a man who was just then passing. The slater did not seriously⁸ injure⁹ himself, but unfortunately¹⁰ killed¹¹ the man. The son of the man killed¹² sued¹³ the slater, and he had to appear¹⁴ at court.¹⁵ Although the slater's innocence¹⁶ was clearly proved,¹⁷ this son used¹⁸ all his influence¹⁹ in order to have him severely punished.²⁰ It was a hard case for the judge to decide²¹ ; but when the son spoke²² of the law of retaliation, he (the judge) sentenced²³ the slater to place²⁴ himself exactly²⁵ on the same spot²⁶ where the old man had stood when the accident²⁷ occurred, and ordered²⁸ the son to climb²⁹ on the roof, then to throw himself down upon him and kill him, if he could.³⁰

¹ Gefeß (n., pl. -e). ² Wiedervergeltung (f.). ³ Schieferdecker (m.). ⁴ arbeiten (reg.). ⁵ high, hoch oben. ⁶ Dach (n., pl. Dächer). ⁷ gleiten (irr.). ⁸ ftart, ernftlich. ⁹ to injure one's self, fich verleßen (reg.). ¹⁰ unglücklicherweife. ¹¹ töten (reg.). ¹² Adj. precedes the noun. ¹³ verflagen (reg.). ¹⁴ erfcheinen (reg.). ¹⁵ vor Gericht or auf dem G. ¹⁶ Unfchuld (f.). ¹⁷ beweifen (irr.). ¹⁸ brauchen (reg.), anwenden (sep., irr.). ¹⁹ Einfluß (m.). ²⁰ ftrafen (reg.). ²¹ entfcheiden (insep., irr.). ²² to speak of, fprechen von (dat., irr.). ²³ verurteilen. ²⁴ fich ftellen (reg.). ²⁵ genau. ²⁶ Stelle (f.), Plaß (m., pl. Pläße). ²⁷ Unfall (m., pl. -fälle). ²⁸ befehlen (insep., irr., dat.). ²⁹ flettern (reg.). ³⁰ Subj., impf. tense or pres.

13. The baked¹ Apple.¹

Lafontaine was in the habit² of eating a baked apple every evening.³ One evening⁴ he was called out of his study,⁵ when he had an apple in his hand, and he laid it on the mantelpiece.⁶ During his absence a friend of his came into the room, saw the apple, and ate it. When Lafontaine returned,⁷ he did not find his apple ; but he guessed at⁸ the truth, and cried with feigned⁹ excitement¹⁰: "What has become of¹¹ my apple, which I left here?" "I do not know," said the visitor.¹² "I am pleased to hear that, for I had put¹⁴ poison¹⁵ into it¹⁴ to kill rats," said the author coolly. "Good heavens¹⁶ ! I am poisoned¹⁷ !" cried the friend, exceedingly¹⁸ frightened. "Send quickly for [19] a physician [20]." " Dear friend, calm yourself, [21] I remember now that I forgot this time to put in the poison ; but I am very sorry [22] that it needed [23] a lie [24] to discover [25] the truth," added [26] Lafontaine.

[1] Bratapfel (m., pl. -äpfel). [2] to be in the habit, die Gewohnheit haben. [3] Acc. of definite time. [4] Gen. of indef. time. [5] Studierzimmer (n.). [6] Kaminfuns (m., pl. -e). [7] zurückkommen (sep., irr.); zurückkehren (sep., reg.). [8] to guess at, erraten (insep., irr.). [9] erkünstelt, verstellt. [10] Aufregung (f., pl. -en). [11] what has become of, was ist aus . . . geworden. [12] Besuch (m.). [13] to be pleased, sich freuen. [14] to put into it, hineinthun (sep., irr.). [15] Gift (n., pl. -e). [16] good heavens, Gerechter Himmel. [17] to poison, vergiften (insp., reg.). [18] äußerst. [19] to send for, schicken nach (acc.). [20] Arzt (m., pl. Ärzte). [21] to calm one's self, sich beruhigen (insep., reg.). [22] I am sorry, es thut mir leid. [23] bedürfen (insep., irr. genitive). [24] Lüge (f., pl. -n). [25] entdecken (insep., reg.); ausfinden (sep., irr.). [26] hinzufügen (sep., reg.).

14. The Marquis[1] at[2] the Observatory.[3]

An elegant [4] Marquis was going [5] to conduct [6] some ladies to [7] the Paris [8] Observatory, to see an eclipse of the sun, [9] which a celebrated astronomer was about to observe. [10] The ladies having been rather a long time [11] at [12] their toilet, [13] the party [14] arrived late, and were told at [15] the gate that the phenomenon [16] had [17] passed. [18] " Never mind, [19] ladies," said the Marquis, "let us go up [20] nevertheless, [21] the astronomer is a friend of mine, [22] and I am sure [23] he will [24] begin it again to oblige [25] me."

[1] Marquis. [2] vor, bei (dat.). [3] Sternwarte (f., pl. -n). [4] artig, fein, elegant. [5] to be going, wollen. [6] geleiten (insp., reg.). [7] auf. [8] Pariser (adj., do not decline). [9] eclipse of the sun, Sonnenfinsternis (f.). [10] beobachten (insep., reg.). [11] a long time, lange. [12] bei, über. [13] Anzug (m., pl. -züge), Anziehen (n.). [14] Gesellschaft (f., pl. -en). [15] an (dat.). [16] Phänomen (n.). Erscheinung (f., pl. -en). [17] Subj. mode after indir. speech. [18] vorüber (sein). [19] never mind, es thut nichts, es macht nichts aus. [20] to go up, hinaufgehen (sep., irr.). [21] bennoch. [22] of mine, von mir. [23] gewiß. [24] future tense. [25] verbinden (insep., irr.).

Beantworten Sie die folgenden Fragen schriftlich auf deutsch:

Mit wem wollte ein Marquis auf die Pariser Sternwarte gehen?

Was ist eine Sternwarte?

Warum wollte diese Gesellschaft auf diese Sternwarte gehen?

Was für eine Finsternis wollte der Astronom beobachten?

---

15. A Trait[1] of Frederick II.

Frederick II. was one day writing a letter in his cabinet,[2] and the door being open, he saw one of his pages,[3] who thought himself[4] alone, taking[5] a pinch[6] from[7] His Majesty's snuff-box.[8] The king then asked him if he found it good, but the lad[9] was overwhelmed[10] with confusion[11] at[12] the unexpected[13] question. The king, however,[14] helped him out of his embarrassment, saying: "This snuff-box is too small for both of us,[15] take it and put[16] it into your pocket."

[1] Zug (m., pl. Züge). [2] Kabinet (n., pl. –e), Geschäftszimmer (n.). [3] Diener (m.). [4] sich. [5] taking = take. [6] Prise (f., pl. –n). [7] out of. [8] Schnupftabaksdose (f., pl. –en). [9] Bursche (m., pl. –en). [10] überwältigt, übermannt. [11] von Verwirrung. [12] über (acc.). [13] unerwartet. [14] jedoch. [15] for both of us, für uns beide. [16] stecken (reg.).

Beantworten Sie die folgenden Fragen schriftlich auf deutsch:

Wer war Friedrich der Zweite?

Was wird in dieser Anekdote von ihm erzählt?

Wo schrieb er einen Brief, und was konnte er durch die offene Thür im Vorzimmer (anteroom) sehen?

Wie half der König dem erschrockenen (overwhelmed) Pagen aus seiner Verlegenheit?

Von was sind die Schnupftabaksdosen gewöhnlich gemacht?

---

16. The roguish[1] Peasant Lad.[2]

A gentleman on horse-back[3] came to the edge[4] of a morass[5] which he considered[6] not safe. Seeing a peasant lad, he asked him whether the bog [7] was hard at [8] the bottom. "O yes, quite [9] hard," answered the rogue. The gentleman rode on, [10] but his horse began to sink. "You rascal," [11] cried [12] the horseman to [12] the fellow, "did you not assure me that the swamp was hard at the bottom!" "And that is the truth," answered the lad, "but you are not yet half way [13] to it [14]."

[1] ſchelmiſch. [2] Bauerburſche (m., pl. -en). [3] on horseback, zu Pferde. [4] Raub (m., pl. Räuber). [5] Moraſt' (m., pl. -äſte). [6] halten für (irr.). [7] Sumpf (m., pl. Sümpfe). [8] auf. [9] ganz. [10] to ride on, fortreiten (sep., irr.), bahinreiten (sep., irr.). [11] Schurke (m., pl. -n). [12] to cry to, zuſchreien (sep., irr., dat.). [13] half-way, halb. [14] barauf.

Beantworten Sie die folgenden Fragen auf deutſch:

Kam der Herr in der Anekdote zu Fuße oder zu Pferde an den Moraſt?

Was befürchtete er, als er an den Rand des Sumpfes kam?

Wen fragte er, um Gewißheit über den Zuſtand des Moraſtes zu erlangen?

Gab ihm dieſer Bauerburſche die erwünſchte Antwort?

Würde es ein Vergnügen geweſen ſein, den Boden dieſes Sumpfes mit dem Pferde zu erreichen?

---

17. The Pope [1] and the Chemist. [2]

When an author writes a book, it is usually the custom to dedicate [3] it to some person of high rank. [4] The [5] better known this latter person is, the [5] better may be the sale [6] of the book, and consequently the better it is for the author.

It is now a well [7] known [7] fact [8] that a great many men were trying, especially in the middle ages, [9] to make gold, or, in [10] other words, to find the philosopher's stone. [11] This was especially the case with [12] monks [13] in their cloisters, [14] and many monks, who were then the only [15] chemists, spent [16] almost their life-time [17] with this experiment. [18] It happened once that such a chemist in Italy, who thought that he had found a method [19]

of making gold, had written a book about it, and, hoping to
receive a good reward,[20] had dedicated his book to no less
a [21] man than Pope Leo X. But the Pope, wise man [22] that
he was, instead of sending the desired [23] reward, sent him only
a large empty purse with the following words: — Since he
knew [24] how to make [25] gold, he needed nothing else [26] but [27]
a bag, large and strong, to hold enough of the precious [28]
metal.[29]

[1] Der Papſt. [2] Chemiker. [3] widmen (reg., dat.). [4] Stand (m., pl.
Stände), Rang (m., pl. Ränge). [5] the ... the, je ... deſto. [6] Verkauf
(m., pl. -käufe). [7] well-known, wohlbekannt (adj.). [8] Thatſache (f., –n).
[9] im Mittelalter (n., pl. —). [10] mit. [11] philosophers' stone, Stein der
Weiſen. [12] mit, bei. [13] Mönch (m., pl. -e). [14] Kloſter (m., pl. Klöſter).
[15] einzig (adj.). [16] hinbringen (sep., irr.), verbringen (insep., irr.). [17] Lebenszeit (f., no plur.). [18] Experiment (n., pl. -e). Verſuch (m., pl. -e).
[19] Methode (f., pl. -n). [20] Belohnung (f., pl. -en). [21] no less a, kein ge-
ringerer. [22] wise man that, der weiſe Mann, der. [23] erwünſcht (adj.).
[24] Subj. mode after indirect speech. [25] how one makes gold. [26] nothing
else, ſonſt nichts. [27] als. [28] koſtbar. [29] Metall (n., pl. -e).

---

18. The stupid[1] Servant.

A lady had given orders [2] one day to her servant, to say, if
any one should call,[3] that she was [4] not at home. She asked
then in the evening who had been at [5] the door that day to pay
her a visit. When she heard the name of her sister among the
others, she said: "But, you stupid fellow, I have told you often
I am [6] always at home for my sister." The next day she did
really [7] go out, and, in her absence, her sister called again and
asked if she was at home. The servant promptly [8] replied:
"She is." The lady entered,[9] and being no stranger [10] in the
house, went upstairs [11] where her sister usually was. She went
directly [12] to [13] her room, and not finding her there, searched [14]
the whole house. Finally satisfied [15] that she was not in the
house, she went downstairs [16] again, and said to the servant:
"My sister is most certainly [17] not in the house — she has very

likely [18] gone out." "That she has [19]," was the reply, "but she told me she was [20] always at home for you."

[1] dumm, albern, einfältig. [2] to give orders, Befehl geben (dat.). [3] vor-sprechen (sep., irr.). [4] Subj. [5] an, vor. [6] Subj. [7] wirklich. [8] schnell, rasch. [9] eintreten (sep., irr.). [10] no stranger, nicht fremd. [11] to go up-stairs, die Treppe hinaufgehen (sep., irr.). [12] direkt, gerade. [13] in. [14] durch-suchen (insep., reg.). [15] überzeugt. [16] to go downstairs, die Treppe hin-untergehen, or heruntergehen (sep., irr.). [17] most certainly, ganz gewiß. [18] very likely, höchst wahrscheinlich. [19] das ist sie. [20] Subj. mode after indirect speech.

19. No Spoon.[1]

Augustus the Strong, King of Saxony, was a great friend of a certain Professor Taubmann. The king invited him to dinner and liked [2] to have sport [3] with him, for the Professor was very witty. He was one day sitting at dinner with the king. Orders had been given that no spoon should be placed [4] before the Professor's soup-plate.[5] When the soup was served and everybody had taken his spoon, the king called out across the table: "A rascal who has no spoon." The Professor said nothing, but took quickly a crust of bread,[6] hollowed [7] it out,[7] stuck [8] it on [8] his fork and, without saying a word, ate his soup with his temporary [9] spoon amidst [10] the laughter [11] of all the guests. When he was ready,[12] he called out just as the king had done [13]: "A rascal who does not eat his spoon," and ate the bread amidst renewed laughter in which even [14] the king joined.[15]

[1] Löffel (m., pl.). [2] gern. [3] Spaß (m., pl. Späße), Scherz (m., pl. -e). [4] legen (reg.). [5] Suppenteller (m., pl.). [6] crust of bread, Brotrinde (f., pl. -n). [7] hollow out, aushöhlen (sep., reg.). [8] to stick on, stecken an (reg.). [9] improvisiert, zeitweilig. [10] unter (dat.). [11] Gelächter (n.). [12] fertig. [13] "had done" is not to be translated. [14] selbst, sogar. [15] einstimmen in (acc., sep., reg.).

20. The Boy and his Father's Hat.

A man with his wife and his little son, about five years old, once made a journey. They travelled by rail.[1] It was a hot

day and the car[2] windows were[3] open. The man made this
journey on business[4] and talked over[5] with his wife the matter[6]
on hand,[7] while his little son amused[8] himself by looking out
of a window, wondering[9] at the new sights.[10] At times he
would put[n] his head out[11] too far, and his father feared that he
might be hurt[12] or that the draught[13] of air might blow off[14]
his hat.[15] He warned[16] him several times, but the little fellow
would not heed[17] him. Finally the father snatched[18] the hat
from the boy's head, hid[19] it and said that[20] the wind had taken
it and that it was now lost.| The boy felt[21] very bad[21] about[21]
his loss, he cried[22] and could not be pacified.[23] After a time
his father told him to be quiet; he would whistle[24] and the
hat would come back again. He did whistle and slyly[25] put[26]
the hat on the boy's head. The boy was then satisfied and sat
quite still for a time. All at once,[27] however, he snatched[28] his
father's hat, threw it out of the window, and said with delight[29]:
" Now, father, whistle, it will come right[30] back again."

[1] by rail, mit ber Eifenbahn. [2] Wagen (m., pl. —). [3] to be open,
offen fein, offen ftehen (irr.). [4] in Geſchäften. [5] to talk over, beſprechen
(insep., irr.), ſprechen von (dat.), über (acc.). [6] Angelegenheit (f., pl. –en).
[7] vorliegend (adj.). [8] to amuse one's self, ſich unterhalten (insep.,
irr.), ſich die Zeit vertreiben ... bamit, baß. [9] ſich wundern über. [10] Ausſicht
(f., pl. –en), Erſcheinung (f., pl. –en). [11] to put out, hinausſtecken (sep.,
reg.), or hinausſtrecken (sep., reg.). [12] verletzen (passive). [13] Luftzug (m.,
pl. –züge). [14] to blow off, wegblaſen (sep., irr.). [15] his hat = him (dat.)
the hat. [16] warnen (reg.). [17] beachten (insep., reg., acc.). [18] to snatch
from, reißen von (irr.). [19] to hide, verſtecken (insep., reg.). [20] said that
(introducing indirect speech, hence subj. mode after it). [21] to feel bad
about, traurig ſein über (acc.). [22] weinen (reg.). [23] beruhigt (passive),
zufrieden geſtellt. [24] pfeifen (irr.). [25] unbemerkt, im Geheimen. [26] ſetzen
auf. [27] auf einmal. [28] herunterreißen (sep., irr.). [29] mit Ergötzen (n., pl.),
Freude (f., pl. –n). [30] ſogleich, ſofort.

---

21. Learning.[1]

A rich farmer's[2] only son, who was studying[3] at[4] a university[5] not many miles away,[6] came home at[7] Christmas to visit

his parents [8] during the holidays.[9] As father, mother and son were sitting at table [10] one evening, the student,[11] wishing to show his learning, said, as two nice fowl [12] were served, that he could, through logic [13] and arithmetic,[14] prove [15] that these two birds were three. "Well, let us hear your proof[16]," said the father. "This," said the learned [17] son, "is one, and this makes two, and you know, of course, that two and one are three, are they not [18]?" "Well said [19]," replied the father, "and since you have made [20] that out [20] so well, and proved it so clearly,[21] your mother shall [22] have one bird, I will take the second, and you shall have the third one for your astonishing [23] wisdom."

[1] Gelehrſamkeit (f., pl. –en). [2] Bauer (m., pl. -n), Farmer (m.). [3] ſtu-bieren (reg., p. p. ſtubiert). [4] auf. [5] Univerſität (f., pl. -en). [6] some miles away, einige Meilen entfernt. [7] at Christmas, zu Weihnachten. [8] Eltern (pl.). [9] Feiertag (m., pl. –e). [10] at table, bei Tiſche. [11] Stu-dent' (m., pl. -en). [12] Hühnchen (n., pl. —). [13] Logik (f., or with article). [14] Arithmetik (f., or with article). [15] beweiſen (insep., irr.). [16] Beweis (m., pl. -ſe). [17] gelehrt (adj.). [18] nicht wahr. [19] ſchön geſagt; vortrefflich. [20] to make out, ausmachen (sep., reg.). [21] klar, deutlich. [22] ſoll. [23] er-ſtaunlich.

22. The Conqueror[1] and the Old Man.

Conqueror. — "Old man, are you[2] deaf[3]?"

Old man. — "Did any one speak?"

C. — "I have lost my way.[4] Lead[5] me out of this wood and I will give yóu this gold-piece."

O. m. — "Wait until I ask[6] you for it, my friend!"

C. — "Am I not known to you?"

O. m. — "I cannot say that I ever saw you before. But, then, my eyesight[7] is none of the best[8]."

C. — "If my face is not known to you, my history[9] must be. For[10] twenty years the world has been filled with my glory[11]."

O. m. — "Glory is a fine thing, but I do not covet[12] it."

C. — "I am the great conqueror: he who conquered so many nations, and shed[13] so much blood[14]."

O. m. — "Well, friend conqueror, this is the first time [15] I ever heard of you."

C. — "Can that be true?"

O. m. — "I hope I do not offend [16] you. How are [17] all the folks at home?"

C. — "It is more than a year [18] now since I conquered this country in which you live, and drove out [19] the king."

O. m. — "So, the old king has gone [20]? Well, he never did me any harm [21] that I know of [22]."

C. — "What have you been about [23] all [24] your life, that you have not heard of these things?"

O. m. — "What have I been about? I have cut [25] down trees, pulled [26] up stumps [27] and stones, planted corn, fed [28] my family, and taught [29] them to do justice, [30] and live uprightly [31]."

C. — "I see how it is, old man. You, too, have been a sort [32] of conqueror."

O. m. — "Yes, I have conquered [33] the stones and stumps; but, I thank the Lord, [34] I have never stained [35] my hand with the blood of my brother-man [36]."

C. — "We will not talk of that. Have you a large family?"

O. m. — "I have a wife, three sons and a daughter. Also a cow, [37] and more hens and chickens than I have counted."

C. — "Are you contented [38]?"

O. m. — "Why not? We have our health [39] and strength, [40] shelter [41] and food, [42] with happy thoughts and trust [43] in [44] heaven."

C. — "Oh, fortunate old man! The world's conqueror has no more than these. No more, did I say? Ah! he has not so much as these!"

---

[1] Eroberer (m., pl. —). [2] Use the second person sing. throughout. [3] taub. [4] to lose one's way, sich verirren. [5] führen (reg.). [6] to ask for, bitten um. [7] Gesicht (n., pl. -e or -er). [8] none of the best, keines von den besten, or nicht vom besten. [9] Geschichte (f., pl. —en). [10] seit (dat.). [11] Ruhm (m.). [12] begehren (insep., reg.). [13] vergießen (insep., irr.). [14] Blut (n.). [15] first time that. [16] beleidigen (insep., reg.). [17] how are, wie

befinden sich. ¹⁸ more than a year, mehr als ein Jahr her, or über ein
Jahr. ¹⁹ to drive out, vertreiben (insep., irr.). ²⁰ fort. ²¹ he never did,
etc., er hat mir nie etwas zu leibe gethan (or kränken, reg.). ²² that I
know. ²³ to be about=to do. ²⁴ all your life, your whole life. ²⁵ to cut
down, fällen (reg.). ²⁶ to pull up, ausrotten (sep., reg.). ²⁷ Stumpf (m.,
pl. Stümpfe). ²⁸ ernähren (insep., reg.). ²⁹ to teach, lehren (reg., acc.),
unterrichten (insep., reg.). ³⁰ Gerechtigkeit (f.). ³¹ ehrlich. ³² a sort of,
eine Art Eroberer. ³³ erobern (reg.). ³⁴ Gott, Herr, himmlischer Vater.
³⁵ beflecken (insep., reg.). ³⁶ Nebenmensch (m., pl. -en). ³⁷ Kuh (f., pl. Kühe).
³⁸ zufrieden. ³⁹ Gesundheit (f.). ⁴⁰ Stärke (f.), Kraft (f., pl. Kräfte). ⁴¹ Ob-
dach (n.). ⁴² Nahrung (f.). ⁴³ Vertrauen (n.). ⁴⁴ auf (acc.).

23. The Conscientious[1] Lady and the Prisoner.[2]

A certain lady was an active[3] and conscientious member[4] of
every philanthropic[5] society[6] wherever[7] (there) was one. She
visited every public[8] institution[9] of the city and the state to see
if she could do any[10] good to[11] some[12] deserving[13] fallen[14] indi-
vidual,[15] be it[16] man, woman or child. She was very wealthy,
and visited the poor in the almshouses[17] and elsewhere[18]; did a
great deal for the comfort[19] of suffering[20] humanity,[21] and gave
much consolation[22] in general.[23] So, one day, she went for the
same purpose[24] to a state prison.[25] Here she noticed, among
a great many hard-looking[26] prisoners, a young man, who
seemed to be, as regards looks,[27] an exception[28] to the rest.[29]
He was quite young, neatly[30] enough dressed,[31] as far as his
prison-garb would allow,[32] and innocent-looking.[33] She asked[34]
of the warden permission to speak with this prisoner. She said
to him kindly[35]: "Young man, what brings you here[36]?" "I
was arrested whilst I was selling Bibles on the street," was the
answer. "Why,[37] that is shocking[38]!" said she; "has it
become a crime[39] to sell that good book on the street?"
"Well," said the young, harmless[40]-looking prisoner, "I was
trying to sell a bible to[41] a lady. I showed her a very beautiful
one, and was urging[42] her to take[43] it, when an officer came[44]
up, laid his hand on my shoulder,[45] and arrested me." "And

where did you buy your bibles?" she asked him. "Oh," was his cool reply, "I had stolen⁴⁶ the bibles."

¹ gewiſſenhaft. ² Gefangene (decl. like an adj.). ³ thätig, wirkſam. ⁴ Mitglied (n., pl. –er). ⁵ menſchenfreundlich. ⁶ Geſellſchaft (f., pl. –en). ⁷ wo nur immer. ⁸ öffentlich. ⁹ Anſtalt (f., pl. –en). ¹⁰ some good, Gutes ("some" and "any" before a noun, in the singular, are very rarely, if·ever, translated). ¹¹ Dative. ¹² irgend ein. ¹³ verdienſtvoll. ¹⁴ (gefallen) geſunken (adj.). ¹⁵ Individuum (n.)., Perſon (f., pl. –en). ¹⁶ ſei es. ¹⁷ Armenhaus (n., pl. –häuſer). ¹⁸ anderswo. ¹⁹ Hülfe (f.). ²⁰ leidend (adj.). ²¹ Menſchheit (f.). ²² Troſt (m.). ²³ im Allgemeinen. ²⁴ for the, etc., in derſelben Abſicht. ²⁵ to a, etc., in ein Staatsgefängnis (n., pl. –ſſe). — The preposition "to" before a person = zu; as, zu meinem Freund. Before a city or country = nach; as, nach Berlin. Before a building, meaning "into it,"= in; as, "to school," in die Schule; before any other place = an; as, "to the river," an den Fluß; an den Tiſch, an das Fenſter. ²⁶ abſtoßend (adj.). ²⁷ was das Ausſehen anbetrifft. ²⁸ Ausnahme (f., pl. –en). ²⁹ von den Übrigen. ³⁰ nett. ³¹ gekleidet. ³² as far as ... would allow, ſo weit ſeine Gefängnis-Tracht es erlaubte. ³³ unſchuldig ausſehend. ³⁴ she asked of the warden permission, ſie bat den Aufſeher um Erlaubnis. ³⁵ freundlich. ³⁶ hierher. ³⁷ Ei! ³⁸ ſchrecklich. ³⁹ Verbrechen (n., pl. —). ⁴⁰ harmlos. ⁴¹ Dative. ⁴² I was urging her, ich drang in ſie. ⁴³ to buy. ⁴⁴ to come up, herzukommen (sep., irr.). ⁴⁵ Schulter (f., pl. –n). ⁴⁶ ſtehlen (irr.).

24. The Likeness.[1]

Many hundred years ago there died, in a large city, a merchant, who left[2] considerable[3] property. It was well known that he had an only son. But this son had left[4] home[5] long ago[6] to travel,[7] and nobody knew him by sight.[8] It was advertised[9] in the papers,[10] as is usual in such cases,[11] and after a time three young men appeared[12] in the city, and each asserted[13] that he was[14] the son and the rightful[15] heir.[16] The judge, Solomon by name,[17] was in doubt[18] what to do.[19] Finally he ordered[20] a picture to be brought,[21] in[22] which the resemblance[23] to the father was striking,[24] and said to the three young men: "He of you that can hit[25] with an arrow[26] the mark[27] which I here make upon the breast of this picture shall be declared[28] the heir[20]." The first one shot, and hit very near the mark; the second hit still[30] nearer; but when the third one took aim,[31] he grew pale,[32] burst into[33] tears,[34] threw bow[35] and arrow on the floor, and cried: "I cannot shoot; I will rather lose the inheritance[36]." "Now," said the judge, "noble youth,[37] you are the true[38] son, and the rightful heir. The other two, who shot so well, are imposters[39]; for, a genuine[40] son can, not even[41] in a picture, pierce[42] the heart of his father with an arrow."

[1] Bildnis (n., pl. -ffe). [2] hinterlaffen (insep., irr.). [3] anfehnlich. [4] verlaffen (insep., irr.). [5] Heimat (f., pl. -en). [6] long ago, fchon lange, vor langer Zeit. [7] to travel, auf Reifen gehen. [8] by sight, von Angeficht. [9] bekannt machen. [10] Zeitung (f., pl. -en). [11] as is, etc. = wie gewöhnlich in folchen Fällen. [12] erfcheinen (insep., irr.). [13] behaupten (insep., reg.). [14] Subj. mode after indirect speech. [15] rechtmäßig. [16] Erbe (m., pl. -n). [17] Namens. [18] in Zweifel. [19] what he should do, was er thun follte. (In English the infinitive after the three words, "how, what, where," must, in German, form a complete clause with the auxiliaries follen, müffen, or können; as, "show him how to do it," zeigen Sie ihm, wie er es thun foll, etc.). [20] befehlen (insep., irr.). [21] a picture to be brought = that a picture should be brought, or ließ ein Bild bringen. [22] auf. [23] Ähnlichkeit (f., pl. -en). [24] fchlagend, auffallend. [25] treffen (irr.). [26] Pfeil (m., pl. -e). [27] Zeichen (n., pl. —). [28] erklären (insep., reg.). [29] als Erbe. [30] noch näher. [31] to take aim, zielen (reg.). [32] to grow pale, erblaffen (insep., reg.). [33] to burst into, ausbrechen in (sep., irr.). [34] Thräne (f., pl. -en). [35] Bogen (m., pl. Bögen). [36] Erbfchaft (f., pl. -en). [37] edler Jüngling. [38] wahr. [39] Betrüger (m., pl. —). [40] echt. [41] not even, fogar nicht or felbft nicht. [42] durchbohren (insep., reg.).

---

25. Disappointed[1] Hope.

A conjurer[2] came to[3] the court of a prince, and asked[4] his permission[4] to show him a trick[5] which he had[6] never yet seen. The prince, who was a kind man, and knew how to appreciate[7] unusual[8] skill,[9] granted the request. The juggler came into the presence[10] of the king with a dish of green peas in his hand. An assistant[11] accompanied him, and when everything was ready, held a needle[12] before the juggler, who then threw the peas with such a certainty[10] that they every time stuck[14] on the point[15] of the needle. The prince expressed[16] his satisfaction,[17] and said: "You had a singular[18] idea,[19] and it must be rewarded[20] in[21] a singular way.[21] Wait here a little, and my servant will bring you what I have destined[22] for you;" and with these words he left the room. Soon the servant came, and gave the juggler a purse. Full[23] of joyous[24] hope, he opened it quickly, but found, to his astonishment,[25] nothing but[26] peas. The juggler, amazed[27] at[28] such an insult,[29] asked what he should do with them. "Very likely continue your studies[30]," answered the king's servant; "our prince generally rewards richly only that which is of advantage[31] to[32] his people, and that is certainly not the case with your art[33]."

[1] vereitelt. [2] Taschenspieler (m.). [3] an. [4] to ask permission, um die Erlaubnis bitten. [5] Kunststück (n.). [6] Subj. after indirect way of speaking. [7] how to appreciate, etc. = how one should, etc.; to appreciate, schätzen (reg.). [8] ungewöhnlich, selten. [9] Geschicklichkeit (f., pl. -en). [10] into the presence, vor (acc.). [11] Gehülfe (m.). [12] Nadel (f.). [13] Sicherheit (f.). [14] stecken bleiben. [15] Spitze (f.). [16] äußern (reg.). [17] Zufriedenheit (f.). [18] sonderbar. [19] Idee (f.). [20] belohnen (insep., reg.). [21] in ... way, in ... manner, auf ... Weise, auf ... Art. [22] bestimmen (insep., reg.). [23] voll (with gen.), or von (dat.). [24] freudig. [25] Erstaunen (n.). [26] als (after "nothing" and "nowhere" "but" is always translated als). [27] erstaunt, entrüstet. [28] über (acc.). [29] Schimpf (m.). [30] Studium (n., pl. Studien). [31] of advantage, von Nutzen. [32] für (or was seinem Volk Nutzen bringt). [33] Kunst (f.).

26. Presence of Mind.[1]

A surgeon had to bleed[2] the Sultan of Turkey. By accident the point of the lancet broke, remained in the vein,[3] and stopped[4] the flow of blood. The question now was how[5] to expel[6] the obstruction[7] quickly. The Æsculapius did not lose his head at this critical moment. He gave his highness[8] a slap[9] in the face, which, through the start[10] caused by the surprise[11] and indignation,[12] assisted the flow of blood, and this caused the expulsion[13] of the obstruction. However, when the attendants[14] were about to seize him, he said: "Leave me alone[15] until I have finished the bleeding,[16] and have bandaged[17] the wound." That operation[18] terminated,[19] he threw himself at the Sultan's feet,[20] and explained the fact.[21] The Sultan pardoned[22] him, and rewarded[23] him for having[24] saved his life by retaining[25] his presence of mind in such a danger.

[1] Geistesgegenwart. [2] zur Aber laſſen (followed by the dat. of person). [3] Aber (f., pl. –n). [4] verhindern (reg.). [5] how to, etc., how he should. [6] heraustreiben (sep., irr.). [7] Verſtopfung (f., pl. –en), Hemmung (f., pl. –en). [8] Hoheit (f., pl. –en), Majeſtät (f., pl. –en). [9] Schlag (m., pl. Schläge), Streich (m., pl. –e). [10] Schreck (m.). [11] Erſtaunen (n.). [12] Entrüſtung (f., pl. –en). [13] Austreibung (f., pl. -en. — The pupil will have noticed that all derivative nouns with the final syllables, ei, heit, keit, ſchaft, ung and in, are of the feminine gender). [14] Dienerſchaft (f., pl. –en), Gefolge (n.). [15] to leave alone, in Frieden laſſen, in Ruhe laſſen, gehen laſſen. [16] Aberlaß (m.). [17] verbinden (insep., irr.). [18] Operation (f., pl. –en). — Nouns of foreign origin ending in ie, ion, it, tät, are of the feminine gender). [19] beendigen (insep., reg.). [20] at the Sultan's, etc. = to the Sultan (dat.) at the feet, dem Sultan zu Füßen. — This dative is used similar to the "Dative of Interest," as: Er gab es mir in die Hand, he gave it me into the hand. [21] Umſtand (m., pl. -ſtände). [22] verzeihen (insep., irr., dat.). [23] Belohnung (insep., reg.). [24] for having = that he had saved. [25] retaining, beibehalten (partly sep., partly insep.); behalte bei, behielt bei, beibehalten or behalten; by retaining, dadurch, daß er . . . beibehielt; or behaupten (insep., reg.).

27. The Duke of Marlborough and the French Prisoner.

The Duke of Marlborough noticed the very handsome[1] form[2] and warlike[3] appearance[4] of one of the prisoners he had taken[5] at[6] Hochstädt. This battle was fought[7] in 1704, between England and France. The English historians[8] however, call it the battle of Blenheim, which latter name is correct enough, according to[9] the situation[10] of the two places.

But to come back[11] to the English general and the French prisoner. The general, as said above,[12] was so much pleased[13] with the manly appearance of the Frenchman, that he could not help[14] making the following flattering remark: "If the French had had 50,000 such men as you are, we should not have gained the day so easily." The Frenchman replied quickly: " By Jove,[15] general, our army has many men like me[16]; we only want[17] one like you."

This answer was no doubt[18] a good one. But what can have been the reason that the Frenchman made[19] it? Did hë perhaps think he might, through this flattery, turn[20] the Duke's good-will[21] in his favor[20]?

[1] anſehnlich. [2] Geſtalt (f., pl. –en). [3] kriegeriſch. [4] Äußere (n.), Ausſehen (n.). [5] to take, gefangen nehmen (irr.). [6] bei. [7] ſchlagen (irr.). [8] Geſchichtſchreiber. [9] nach (dat.), gemäß, zu Folge. [10] Lage (f., pl. –n). [11] to come back to, zurückkommen auf (sep., irr.). [12] oben. [13] erfreut über. [14] cannot help, nicht umhin können; ich kann nicht umhin . . . zu. [15] Beim Jupiter, beim Zeus. [16] like me = as I, wie ich (bin). [17] uns fehlt. [18] ohne Zweifel. [19] geben. [20] to turn in his favor = ſich zu Gunſten wenden. [21] Wohlwollen (n.).

---

28. One Smaller than the Other.

Now-a-days,[1] when a man, a woman or a child wants a pair of boots or shoes, he usually goes to a shoe-store and buys ready-made[2] whatever[3] he wants in this line.[4] But years ago it was different. There were no ready-made shoes in those days, and people always went to a shoemaker, who took their measure,[5] and then made the article.[6]

Now it happened once that a farm-laborer[7] needed a pair of boots. He went, therefore, to the right place, and ordered[8] a pair of strong cow-hide[9] boots. When the shoemaker had taken the measure, the laborer remarked, as he was on the point of going, that one of his feet was a trifle[10] larger than the other, and that he wanted the boots made accordingly.[11] The shoemaker, having finished[12] the boots, brought them to the customer,[13] who tried[14] them on[14] at once. Fortunately,[15] or unfortunately, as you will, the laborer put[16] the larger boot on the smaller foot, and everything went well enough. But, alas ! when it was the other foot's turn,[17] i. e. when he wanted to put the smaller boot on the larger foot, all efforts[18] were in vain,[19] and he angrily said to the shoemaker, who was looking on in silence[20] : "I told you to make one boot larger than the other, and now, you can see it yourself, you have made one smaller than the other."

[1] heutzutage. [2] fertig gemacht. [3] was. [4] Art (f., pl. –en), Beziehung (f., pl. –en). [5] Maß (n., pl. –e). [6] Artikel (m.). [7] farm-laborer, Bauer (m., pl. –n). [8] bestellen (insep., reg.). [9] rindledern. [10] a trifle, ein wenig. [11] demgemäß. [12] fertig haben, machen (reg.). [13] Kunde (m., pl. –n). [14] to try on, anprobieren (reg.; verbs ending in ieren are derived from foreign languages; they are, as a rule, regular, but they omit ge in the past part.). [15] glücklicherweise. [16] ziehen an. [17] wenn die Reihe am andern Fuße war, or wenn die Reihe an den andern Fuß kam. [18] Bemühung (f., pl. –en). [19] umsonst, vergeblich, fruchtlos. [20] stillschweigend.

29. Your Hand is larger than Mine.

One afternoon in summer a mother and her little daughter, Anna, were sitting in their sitting-room.[1] It was a plain room, with nothing unusual[2] in it. In the centre[3] was a round table, — a wooden frame[4] with a marble slab,[5] — such as may be seen[6] almost anywhere. Upon this table stood two common porcelain[7] plates; on one were some apples, upon the other raisins. Besides[8] this table there were a sofa,[9] and half a dozen[10] chairs covered[11] with hair-cloth[12]; on the walls[13] were hanging a few cheap but nice pictures, and a map[14] of the United States.[15] The mother sat in[16] one of the chairs at the window, and was sewing[17] on a new summer-dress for her daughter. Little Anna[18] sat, or rather[19] kneeled,[20] in a corner on the carpet, and played and talked in a child-like way with her doll,[21] as if it were really[22] a little living being.[23] Finally, when she was tired[24] of playing,[25] she arose, and her eyes[26] fell accidently upon the fruit on the table. She wanted[27] some raisins, and therefore asked her mother to give her a handful[28]; but her mother, being busy with sewing, told her to take a handful herself. Upon this Anna said: "Will you not give me the raisins yourself?" Her

mother then wished to know why she would not help[29] herself.
Little Anna looked at her mother with eyes half cast down,[30] as
if in expectation[31] of what[32] her mother would say to her reply,
and said: "Ah, dear mother, pray[33] give me a handful of
raisins; you know your hand is larger than mine."

[1] Wohnzimmer (neut.). [2] Ungewöhnliches (decl. like an adj.). [3] Mitte
(f., no plur.). [4] Gestell (n.). [5] Marmorplatte (f., pl. -n). [6] such as may
be seen = as one can see, wie man sehen kann. [7] Porzellanteller (m.).
[8] außer (prep., dat.). [9] Sopha, or Sofa (n., pl. -s). [10] half a dozen, ein
halbes Dutzend. [11] überzogen (from überziehen). [12] Haartuch (n., pl. -e).
[13] Wand (f., pl. Wände). [14] Laubkarte (f., pl. -n). [15] Die Vereinigten
Staaten. [16] auf. [17] nähen. [18] the little Anna (any proper name preceded by an adj. must use the definite article). [19] vielmehr. [20] knien
(reg., better than knieen). [21] Puppe (f., pl. -n). [22] wirklich. [23] Wesen
(n., pl. —), or Geschöpf (n., pl. -e). [24] müde (adj., governing the gen. case
and follows its object). [25] Spielen (n.). [26] Auge (f., pl. -n), Blick (m.,
pl. -e). [27] She wanted, sie wollte haben, sie wünschte. [28] Handvoll (f.).
[29] to help one's self, zulangen. [30] to cast down, niederschlagen (sep.,
irr.); with eyes half cast down = with half cast down eyes. [31] Erwar-
tung (f., pl. -en). [32] of what = what. [33] bitte (ich bitte).

---

80. Cunning.[1]

A rich nobleman missed[2] from his dining-room[3] at his coun-
try-seat[4] a great deal of silverware.[5] There was no other way to
account for[6] his loss than to say that[7] somebody had stolen it.
The question now was, who was the thief? A stranger could[8]
not very well have come[8] into the house in the day-time,[9] without being seen by some of the domestics; and by night it was
still less possible,[10] for windows and doors were securely[11] locked
and bolted,[12] and, besides,[13] there was always a large, ferocious[14]
dog around the house. So one among the servants in the house
must be the thief. But all endeavors to get upon the track of
the guilty one[15] were fruitless. Finally something occurred to
the nobleman which, he thought, would have the desired effect.[16]
For this purpose[17] he one evening summoned[18] to his room all
whom he suspected,[19] and addressed[20] them in the following

manner: "Among you is most certainly the one who stole my silverware, and I (shall) now positively[11] detect[22] him." In order to make his plan work well, he ordered his servants to stand around a large table, which stood in the centre of the room; then he worked out his plan. First he muttered[23] all sorts of[24] unintelligible[25] words, and, at the same time, struck with a short, black stick now[26] upon the table before him, then[26] about him; then he ordered his servants to hold up[27] now one, now the other, hand, then both; or to stand upon one leg, or to stoop. Finally, when he thought that, through his words, intelligible as well as unintelligible, he had directed[28] their whole attention[29] upon[28] his hocus pocus,[30] he believed it was time to strike the decisive blow.[31] He therefore ordered them, one and all,[32] to put[33] their heads under the table. This being done, he asked quickly, not giving them any time for consideration[34]: "Are you ready? Have you your heads under the table?" They all, to a man,[35] promptly replied "Yes, sir." He followed quickly with his final question: "The thief also?" And, sure enough,[36] he succeeded in his plan.[37] The coachman,[38] big fool[39] that he was, answered: "Yes, sir."

---

[1] Lift (f.). [2] vermiffen (insep., reg.). [3] dining-room, Speifezimmer (n.). [4] Landhaus (n.). [5] Silbergerät (n., pl. -e). [6] to account for, erflären (insep., reg.). [7] than to say that = than that, als daß. [8] could have come, hätte kommen können. [9] zur Tageszeit (f., pl. -en). [10] still less possible, noch weniger möglich. [11] ficher, feft. [12] verriegeln (insep., reg.). [13] außerdem (adv.). [14] grimmig. [15] to get upon the track of the guilty one, dem Schuldigen auf die Spur zu kommen. [16] Wirfung (f., pl. -en). [17] in diefer Abficht. [18] to summon, rufen laffen. [19] in Verdacht haben. [20] anreden (sep., reg.). [21] ficherlich, abfolut. [22] entdecken (insep., reg.). [23] brummen (reg.). [24] allerlei. [25] unverftändlich. [26] now ... then, bald ... bald. [27] to hold up, in die Höhe zu halten. [28] to direct upon, richten auf (reg.). [29] Aufmerffamfeit (f., pl. -en). [30] Hofus-Pofus (m.). [31] to strike the decisive blow, den entfcheidenden Schlag zu thun. [32] one and all, alle und jeder, männiglich. [33] ftecken (reg.). [34] zur Überlegung (f.), Erwägung (f., pl. -en). [35] to a man = to the last man, bis auf den letzten Mann. [36] sure enough, ganz gewiß, richtig, wahrlich, wahrhaftig. [37] to succeed in his plan, der Plan gelang ihm, es gelang ihm mit dem Plan; es gelingt mir, I succeed. [38] Kutfcher (m.). [39] big fool = the big fool, der große Narr.

31. Elizabeth's Death.

False reports[1] of the death of Elizabeth, Queen of England, had often been spread[2] about. A magistrate[3] of a city in England, who had several times been deceived[4] by these rumors, said at last, that he would never believe the report until he saw it signed[5] under her own hand.[6]

Well said, faithful[7] subject,[8] to believe in[9] the infallible[10] and ruling[11] hand of thy sovereign[12]; but, remember, it is best to think first, and then to speak or act.[13]

[1] Gerücht (n., pl. -e). [2] to be spread about, sich verbreiten (reg.). [3] Magistratsperson. [4] täuschen (reg.). [5] unterschreiben (insep., irr.). [6] under her own hand, eigenhändig (von ihr). [7] getreu. [8] Unterthan (n., pl. -en). [9] an (acc.). [10] unfehlbar. [11] ordnend, entscheiden. [12] Landesherr (m., pl. -en), Landesfürst (m., pl. -en). [13] handeln (reg.).

32. Except[1] the Mayor.

Foote, the great English comic actor,[2] was travelling one day in the west[3] of England, and dined at an inn. When the cloth[4] was removed,[4] the landlord asked him, how he liked[5] his dinner. "I have dined as well as any man in old England," answered Foote. "Except the mayor," cried the host. "I don't except[6] anybody whatever[7]," said Foote. "But you must!" bawled[8] the host again. "I wont[9]!" "You must!" At length the landlord, who was a petty magistrate,[10] ended the strife by taking Foote before the mayor, who observed that it had been customary in that town for a great number of years[11] always to except the mayor; so[12] he fined[13] the actor one shilling.[14] Upon this decision,[15] Foote paid the shilling, and remarked at the same time, that he thought[16] the landlord the greatest fool in Christendom,[17] except the Mr. Mayor.

[1] ausgenommen (past part.). [2] Komiker. [3] im Westen. [4] to remove the cloth, abdecken. [5] gefallen (insep., irr.). [6] ausnehmen (sep., irr.). [7] durchaus. [8] schreien (irr.). [9] I will not. [10] kleiner Beamter. [11] for a great etc. eine große Anzahl von Jahren, or seit vielen Jahren. [12] demzufolge, folglich. [13] strafen (um). [14] Schilling (m., pl. -e). [15] upon this decision, auf diese Entscheidung hin. [16] halten für (acc.). [17] Christenheit (f.).

33.

BOSTON, May 12th, 1882.[1]

My dearest Cousin[2]!

I am exceedingly[3] grateful[4] to you for the complete[5] and very interesting description[6] you gave me in your last letter, of the different cities and places, especially in Germany, where you have been stopping[7] during your sojourn[8] in Europe. But, most of all,[9] I thank you for your kind invitation[10] to stay[11] with[12] you.

Your full description of that country and its people[13] has aroused[14] my desire to go to such a degree,[15] that I can no longer resist[16] your well-meant[17] wish and offer.[18]

I only needed to decide, for my folks had given me their consent[19] long ago.

Hoping[20] to hear from you soon, believe me,[21]

Your sincere[22] cousin,

N. N.

[1] Boſton, ben zwölften Mai — ben 12ten Mai. [2] Couſine (female cousin). Vetter (male). [3] außerorbentlich. [4] banfbar (dat.). [5] vollſtänbig. [6] Beſchreibung (f., pl. –en). [7] to stop, ſich aufhalten (sep., irr.). [8] Bleiben (n.). [9] am allermeiſten. [10] Einlabung (f., pl. –en). [11] bleiben (irr.). [12] bei. [13] Nation (f., pl. –en), or Leute (pl.). [14] erregen (insep., reg.). [15] Grab (m., pl. –e). [16] wiberſtehen (insep., irr.). [17] wohlgemeint. [18] Anerbieten (n.). [19] Einwilligung (f., pl. –en). [20] in the hope that, in ber Hoffnung, baß. [21] verbleibe ich. [22] aufrichtig.

34.

BERLIN, June 17th, 1882.

My dearest Cousin, Helene !

I cannot in[1] words express[2] with what delight I read that surprising[3] news in your letter. Do come[4] as soon as possible. Bring no unnecessary[5] things with you[6]; at least,[7] do not buy anything new, as gloves, shoes, etc., for you can purchase everything much cheaper here than in America, and things here are certainly[8] as good and as nice as they are there. I wish, however, that you would bring me a few articles, books, etc., a list of which I will send you⁹ the next time¹⁰ I write to you.

How very glad I shall be to introduce¹¹ you to some of the friends I have made here. They are very sociable¹² and pleasant people, and you will be surprised¹³ at seeing in how short a time you will be able to converse¹⁴ with them in German. They are so patient, and take¹⁵ so much pains,¹⁵ and yet they all understand English; in fact,¹⁶ English is taught in the upper¹⁷ classes of all the schools.

My best wishes to¹⁸ our friends, and, most of all, to yourself, from

Yours truly,¹⁹

N. N.

¹ in, mit. ² auśbrüden (reg.). ³ überraſchen (insep., reg.). ⁴ do come, komme ja, or doch. ⁵ unnötig. ⁶ to bring with one's self, mitbringen (irr.). ⁷ wenigſtenś. ⁸ ſicherlich. ⁹ a list of which I will send you = of which I will send you a list, wovon ich dir eine Liſte, etc. ¹⁰ the next time that. ¹¹ vorſtellen (reg., dat.). ¹² geſellig. ¹³ erſtaunt. ¹⁴ ſich unterhalten (mit). ¹⁵ to take much pains, ſich viele Mühe geben. ¹⁶ in der That. ¹⁷ ober (adj.). ¹⁸ an (acc.). ¹⁹ treu.

35.

DRESDEN, July 4th, 1882.

My very dear Cousin!

Shortly¹ after² having written my last letter to you, I made preparations³ for my departure from Berlin to Dresden, where I arrived the day before yesterday.⁴ As the Germans in Dresden do not celebrate⁵ the Fourth of July,⁶ I cannot do it any better⁷ myself than by writing to you.

I found the journey from Berlin to Dresden far less disagreeable than that from Paris to Lyons a year ago. The roads were not so dusty,⁸ on account of⁹ a nice,¹⁰ refreshing¹¹ rain the day previous.¹² On the whole,¹³ the roads here all over the country¹⁴ are made pleasant and cool by¹⁵ the shade-trees, or, in some places, by the fruit-trees which are planted on¹⁶ either¹⁷ side. The country varies [19] between slight [20] elevations [21] and level ground, [22] and is by no means [23] so rocky [24] and mountainous, [25] as that which I saw from Paris to Lyons. The weather was delightful, and just as one would wish it.

I have already paid several visits, and have seen a large part of the city, which I like [26] very much, especially the Altstadt, [27] as it is called, to distinguish [28] it from the Neustadt. [27]

The streets are remarkably [29] clean, very broad and well-paved. [30] The principal street [31] is elegant, and runs [32] from Altstadt to Neustadt across the magnificent [33] bridge of the Elbe. [34]

You will now wonder, how I can be so well acquainted with these localities [35] after a stay of only one week. I owe [36] all this to our friend, Mr. B., who has been kind enough to introduce me to some distinguished [37] people, and to conduct me about town, [38] describing [39] to me everything noteworthy. [40] He has also invited me to dine with his family at his country residence, which stands on an eminence [41] on the banks of the Elbe, and from which, in clear weather, a splendid view [42] may be had [43] for miles around, [44] nearly into Bohemia. If I continue to like Dresden [45] as I do so far, I shall stay here for the rest of my time [46] in Europe, and your next letter, and soon yourself, will in all probability [47] find me at No. 4 Königs-Strasse, 74.

Pray, consider [48] once more my oft repeated [49] request to come, and to spend [50] with me the rest of my stay in Germany.

Please present [51] my best regards [51] to our friends, and take many, many to yourself from

Your most [52] sincere cousin,

N. N.

---

[1] furz. [2] after, nachdem. [3] to make preparations, Vorbereitungen treffen (irr.). [4] the day bef. yesterday, vorgestern. [5] feiern (reg.). [6] der vierte Juli. [7] any better = better. [8] staubig. [9] on account of, wegen (gen.). [10] schön. [11] erfrischend. [12] vorher (adv.). [13] on the whole, im Ganzen genommen, überhaupt. [14] all over the country, durch das ganze Land. [15] durch. [16] an. [17] auf. [18] beide. [19] sich verändern (insep., reg.), abwechseln (sep., reg.). [20] klein. [21] Anhöhe (f., pl. -n). [22] level ground,

Ebene (f., pl. -n). ²³ keineswegs. ²⁴ felfig. ²⁵ gebirgig. ²⁶ gefallen (insep.,
irr.). ²⁷ Altſtadt, Neuſtadt, German words for old and new city. ²⁸ unter=
ſcheiden (insep., irr.). ²⁹ bemerkenswert, beſonders. ³⁰ wohlgepflaſtert.
³¹ Hauptſtraße (f., pl. -n.). ³² laufen (irr.), gehen (irr.). ³³ prächtig, herr=
lich. ³⁴ Elbbrücke (f., pl. -n). ³⁵ Lokalität (f., pl. –en), Örtlichkeit (f., pl.
–en). ³⁶ verbanken (insep., reg, dat. of person). ³⁷ angeſehen, achtbar
(adj.). ³⁸ to conduct about. herumführen in der Stadt. ³⁹ beſchreiben
(insep., irr., dat.). ⁴⁰ beachtenswert. ⁴¹ Erhöhung (f., pl. –en). ⁴² Aus=
ſicht (f., pl. –en). ⁴³ may be had, man kann haben. ⁴⁴ for miles around,
auf Meilen im Umkreis. ⁴⁵ if I continue to like Dresden as I do so far,
wenn mir Dresden ferner gefällt, wie bisher. ⁴⁶ for the rest of my time,
während meiner übrigen Zeit. ⁴⁷ in all probability, aller Wahrſcheinlichkeit
nach. ⁴⁸ erwägen (reg.), bedenken (irr.). ⁴⁹ oft wiederholt. ⁵⁰ zubringen
(sep., irr.). ⁵¹ to present best regards, beſtens grüßen (reg.). ⁵² höchſt.

---

36. Put on[1] your Spectacles.

It has been customary at all times, among[2] all civilized[3]
nations, for every witness[4] at a court of justice[5] to take an oath.[6]
This is done[7] by[8] the witness holding[8] up either his right hand,
or the thumb,[9] the index[10] and the middle finger[11] of his right
hand, while the oath is read[12] to him.   Another manner of
administering the oath[13] is to cause the witness to kiss[14] the
Holy Bible.

It occurred once that a dyer[16] was before a court as a
witness.   He was told to hold up his right hand to take the
usual oath.   His hand, however, was quite black, a natural[17]
consequence[18] of his calling.[19] The judge, being[20] near-sighted,[21]
thought he had on[22] gloves,[23] which is contrary to law,[24] and
told him to take them off.[25] The dyer, not at all[26] slow to
answer, replied : "Put on[27] your spectacles, my lord."— Some
one wondered, what a witness would hold up, if he had been
so unfortunate as to lose both of his[28] hands and arms.

¹ to put on, auffetzen. ² bei. ³ civiliſieren, bilden. ⁴ Zeuge (m.). ⁵ court
of justice, Gericht (n.). ⁶ to take on oath, einen Eid ablegen. ⁷ this is
done, das geſchieht. ⁸ by holding up, in die Höhe halten, or aufheben =
dadurch, daß. ⁹ Daumen (m.). ¹⁰ Zeigefinger (m.). ¹¹ Mittelfinger (m.).

¹² vorlefen (dative). ¹³ ben Eib abnehmen, ſchwören laſſen. ¹⁴ küſſen. ¹⁵ heilige Schrift (f.). ¹⁶ Färber (m.). ¹⁷ natürlich. ¹⁸ Folge (f.). ¹⁹ Beruf (m.). ²⁰ being = who was (see remarks at the end of notes). ²¹ near-sighted, kurzſichtig. ²² to have on, anhaben. ²³ Handſchuh (m., pl. -e). ²⁴ contrary to law, gegen baß Geſetz, or geſetzwibrig (adj.). ²⁵ to take off, ausziehen. ²⁶ not at all slow to answer, burchaus nicht langſam im Antworten. ²⁷ to put on, aufſetzen. ²⁸ both of his = his both.

Remarks on the Present Participle.

a) The English present participle, as has been said above, is expressed in German in various ways. If it replaces a relative pronoun, it must be expressed in German with the verb in the corresponding tense :

1. A man speaking well of everybody.
   Ein Mann, welcher Gutes von jebermann ſpricht.

2. The judge being near-sighted.
   Der Richter, welcher kurzſichtig war.

b) However, the present participle in English is used very frequently by itself, to denote " time, cause or reason " ; in this case it must be replaced by a conjunction and the personal verb.

I. When the present participle expresses time, the conjunctions are als (" when," or " as "), nachbem (" after "), or inbem (" while "), as :

1. Going to Boston I met my friend.
   Als ich nach Boſton ging, begegnete ich meinem Freunbe.

2. Having worked all day he took a walk.
   Nachbem er ben ganzen Tag gearbeitet hatte, ging er ſpazieren.

3. Opening the books, she found her exercise.
   Inbem ſie baß Buch öffnete, fanb ſie ihre Aufgabe.

II. When the present participle expresses a cause or reason, the conjunctions to be used are ba (" as," or " since "), weil (" because "), as :

1. Being sick, he cannot go out.

   Da er frank ist, kann er nicht ausgehen.

2. This being the case, we will not go.

   Da dies der Fall ist, wollen wir nicht gehen.

The progressive form in English, however, does not come under these rules, but is simply expressed by the corresponding finite verb in German, as :

He was going = he went, er ging.

He was writing a letter = he wrote a letter, er schrieb einen Brief.

---

37. General Washington and the Corporal.[1]

During the Revolutionary War[2] of America, a corporal was sent with a little band[3] of soldiers to repair[4] one of the fortifications.[5] A heavy beam was to be raised,[6] the weight of which[7] was beyond their strength,[8] and the corporal could often be heard[9] calling: "Heave away[10]! Now it goes[11]! Heave again!" He was standing there with his hands in his pockets, instead of lending a hand.[12] An officer, not in uniform, was just passing on horseback,[13] and asked the overseer why he did not render a little aid.[14] The latter astonished, turned around with all the pomp of an emperor, and said: "Sir, I am a corporal." "Ah! are you? I beg your pardon, Mr. Corporal, I was not aware[15] of that," said the officer, taking off his hat and bowing.[16] Then, dismounting,[17] he lifted until the perspiration[18] stood in drops on his forehead.

When finally the beam was raised to its position,[19] the officer turned to the great corporal and said: "Mr. Corporal, when you have another such job[20] and have not men enough, send for your commander-in-chief,[21] and I shall gladly come and help you a second time."

Words cannot describe the embarrassment of the corporal, who thus learned that this officer was Gen. Geo. Washington.

[1] Korporal' (m., pl. -e). [2] Revolutions-Krieg (m., pl. -e). [3] Rotte (f., pl. -n), Schar (f., pl. -en), Kompagnie (f., pl. -n), Haufen (m.). [4] ausbessern. [5] Schanze (f., pl. -n). [6] mußte in die Höhe gehoben werden. [7] the weight of which = whose weight, dessen Gewicht, or Schwere. [8] was beyond their strength, ging über ihre Kräfte (pl. of Kraft), or Stärke. [9] could be heard = one could hear. [10] Hebet zu! or Frisch zu! [11] jetzt geht es = geht's. [12] instead of lending a hand, anstatt Hilfe zu leisten, or zu helfen ("instead of lending," see remarks at the end of these notes). [13] to be passing on horseback, vorbeireiten. [14] to render a little aid, ein wenig Hilfe leisten. [15] to be aware of it, es wissen. [16] sich verneigen. [17] absteigen. [18] Schweiß (m.). [19] Platz (m.), Stelle (f.). [20] Arbeit (f.), Geschäft (n.). [21] der Oberbefehlshaber.

Further Remarks on the English Present Participle.

a) When the present participle in English depends upon a verb or a noun, it is rendered in German by the infinitive with zu, as :

> 1. He began writing.
>   Er fing an zu schreiben.
> 2. She stopped singing.
>   Sie hörte auf zu singen.
> 3. The art of painting.
>   Die Kunst zu malen.
> 4. The pleasure of seeing him.
>   Das Vergnügen, ihn zu sehen.

b) When the English present participle is immediately preceded by one of the following words: "instead of" (anstatt), "on, upon, with, without" (ohne), it is translated in German by the corresponding preposition and the infinitive with zu, as :

> 1. He is reading instead of writing.
>   Er liest, anstatt zu schreiben.
> 2. He went away without saying a word.
>   Er ging fort, ohne ein Wort zu sagen.
> 3. He has decided on going into the country.
>   Er hat beschlossen, auf das Land zu gehen.

38. Among Friends any Trifle is of Value.

It is a well-known fact that some people are in the habit of saying for[1] the slightest[2] cause[3] : " I'll bet you[4] !" or " What will you bet?" This habit has become almost an annoyance.[5] The words are used apparently[6] to strengthen some assertion.[7] Not only boys, but even men use the expression, though one would judge[8] that they would have a better idea of propriety.[9] What these people bet varies[10] from five cents to five dollars, or more. And we may hear a little street-urchin[11] say : " I'll bet you five dollars !" when, at the same time, the little fellow never saw or, at least, never possessed[12] that sum of money.

Well, what matters it[13]? The bet would perhaps never be paid, and, moreover,[14] this is the country for betting.[15] But men do not bet money only ; we hear of all sorts[16] of comical bets, especially at election-time.[17] For example : a supper, a new hat, a wheelbarrow ride,[18] etc.

But, proceeding to[19] our real anecdote, we find an amusing[20] result[21] of a betting-affair.[22] It seems that a well-known French philosopher was at one time the president of a philosophical society. A dull[23] member contradicted[24] some assertion he had made, and to make his case more probable,[25] exclaimed: " I'll bet you my head that you are wrong[26]." A wittier answer than the one the president made is not heard every day. " I accept your offer[27]," he replied, "for among friends any trifle is of value." The question arises[28] : Did the shallow[29] member feel the sarcasm?

[1] bei. [2] gering. [3] Gelegenheit (f., pl. –en). [4] I'll bet you! Ich wette (Dir, or Ihnen)! [5] Plage (f., pl. –n), Lästigkeit (f., pl. –en). [6] scheinbar. [7] Behauptung (f., pl. –en). [8] erwarten, urteilen. [9] feeling for propriety, Gefühl für Anstand. [10] wechseln. [11] Straßenläufer (m.), Gassenbube (m., pl. –n). [12] besitzen. [13] what matters it, was macht es aus, was thut es, was liegt daran. [14] überdies. [15] zum Wetten. [16] all sorts, allerlei. [17] zur Zeit der Wahl. [18] Schubkarren=Fahrt (f.). [19] to go over to, übergehen auf. [20] interessant. [21] Resultat (n., pl. –e). [22] Wette (f., pl. –n). [23] geistlos, schwachköpfig. [24] widersprechen (dat.). [25] wahrscheinlich. [26] to be wrong, unrecht haben ; to be right, recht haben. [27] Anerbieten (n.). [28] sein. [29] schal.

39. Shakespeare as a Mimic Monarch.[1]

Shakespeare, the great dramatic writer and actor, was in every respect[2] a great man. We have in his works numberless proofs of his genius, and in his life, of his presence of mind. His life is marked[3] by the most extraordinary events, the most favorable[4] of which was probably that he lived during the reign of Elizabeth, who herself was a most[5] learned woman, and knew how a man like Shakespeare was to be appreciated.

It happened one evening that Shakespeare was playing before the queen the part[6] of a king in one of his tragedies.[7] The queen wished to know if he were true to[8] his character, or whether he could be induced[9] to forget the dignity[10] of the monarch for a moment. She, therefore, dropped her handkerchief, as if by accident,[11] upon the stage at his feet. But the mimic monarch, never losing sight of his character[12] as king, nor wanting in respect to the real queen,[13] spoke, as if nothing outside[14] of the regular part had happened: "However, before this is done,[15] let us pick up[16] the handkerchief of our sister."

This is perhaps the most extraordinary impromptu speech[17] on the stage; every word is in keeping[18] with his genius.

[1] Schauspielerkönig (m., pl. –e). [2] Beziehung (f., pl. –en). [3] ausgezeichnet (durch). [4] günstig. [5] höchst. [6] Rolle (f., pl. –n). [7] Trauerspiel (n., pl. –e), Tragödie (f., pl. –n). [8] true to, getreu (dat.). [9] verleiten, bewegen, veranlassen. [10] Würde (f., pl. –n). [11] als ob durch Zufall. [12] never losing sight of his character, nie die Rolle des Königs aus dem Gesicht verlierend. [13] nor wanting in respect to the real queen, noch gegen den Respekt der wirklichen Königin verstoßend. [14] außerhalb (preposition). [15] geschehen. [16] aufheben, aufnehmen. [17] Worte aus dem Stegreif. [18] im Einklang (m., pl. –klänge).

---

40. Covered with Earth.

A certain doctor in London had the bad[1] habit of never paying his debts,[2] if he could possibly frighten his creditors.[3] It happened that he owed a sum of money to a man who had paved the street before his house. After several fruitless attempts to obtain[4] his pay from the doctor, he caught[5] him one day as he was stepping⁶ from his carriage before his own door, and again demanded⁷ the pay for his work. The doctor, in his usual rough way, tried to frighten him. He called him a rascal and a fraud,⁸ and said that the work was badly done, that the pavement was spoiled,⁹ and then covered with sand and earth, so that it could not be seen, and that he would never pay for such work.

The paver was frightened¹⁰ neither by¹¹ the harsh¹² manner of the doctor, whom he well knew, nor by that of any other person, especially when anybody did him wrong,¹³ as in this case ; so he gave back as much as he had received, by saying : "Doctor ! Mine is not the only bad work that is buried under the earth. Neither does it lie as deep as some."

The doctor was pleased with this ready¹⁴ wit, took him into his office,¹⁵ and paid his bill with good grace.¹⁶

¹übel, böfe. ² Schulden (pl.). ³ Gläubiger. ⁴ erhalten. ⁵ erwifchen. ⁶ fteigen aus. ⁷ fordern. ⁸ Betrüger. ⁹ verderben. ¹⁰ to be frightened, erfchrecken. ¹¹ über. ¹² ftürmifch, laut. ¹³ to do wrong, Unrecht thun. ¹⁴ fchnell. ¹⁵ Privatzimmer. ¹⁶ Anftand (m.).

---

41. The Brave Soldier.

The celebrated English general, Elliot, while inspecting¹ the sentinels one day, during the siege of² Gibraltar, came upon³ a German soldier, who neither "shouldered" nor "presented arms⁴," but stood there⁵ immovable. "Do you not know me, my son?" the general said to the soldier, "or why do you not do⁶ your duty ? "

The soldier answered with self-command⁷: "I know you, general, and my duty very well ; but just now two fingers of my right hand have been shot off, therefore I am not able⁸ to hold the musket." "Why do you not go then, and have⁹ them dressed?" General Elliot continued. "Because," replied the soldier, "in Germany one is not allowed to leave his post until relieved¹¹."

The general immediately dismounted,[12] and said : "Give me your musket and your cartridge-box.[13] I will relieve you that you may[14] have your wound dressed." The soldier obeyed, but went first to the next guardhouse,[15] reported[16] that the general was standing guard,[17] and, not till[18] then, did he have his mutilated[19] hand dressed.

As he was no longer fit for[20] service, he was discharged,[21] and received a considerable[22] present from the general, who sent an account of the incident[23] to London. When the soldier arrived in the capital of England, King George sent for[24] him to come to the palace, gave him a rich reward, and made him an officer for life.[25]

[1] befichtigen, infpicieren (*milit.*). [2] Belagerung (f.) von. [3] to come upon, antreffen (sep., irr.). [4] to shoulder, present arms, das Gewehr fchultern, präfentieren. [5] to stand there, daftehen (sep., irr.). [6] to do thun, (beobachten). [7] Faffung (f.). [8] to be able, im Stande fein. [9] laffen. [10] verbinden. [11] to relieve, ablöfen; until one is relieved (passive voice). [12] abfteigen, or vom Pferde fteigen (irr.). [13] Patrontafche (f.). [14] können. [15] to the guardhouse, auf die Wache. [16] melden. [17] to stand guard, auf Poften ftehen (use subj. mode, impf. tense). [18] not till then, erft dann, or dann erft. [19] verftümmelt. [20] to be fit for, tauglich fein zu. [21] verabfchieden (passive voice). [22] anfehnlich. [23] an account of the incident, ein Bericht über den Vorfall. [24] to send for, fchicken nach. [25] made him an officer for life, machte ihn zum Offizier auf Lebenszeit.

Remarks.

The verbs ernennen, "to appoint," erwählen, "to elect," machen, "to make," govern in the active in English two accusatives ; while in German one object is in the accusative, and the other requires the preposition zu with the dative, as :

He made him an officer, er machte ihn zum Offizier.

More often, however, the passive is used in English with these verbs, governing two nominatives. One then is in German the nominative, as subject of course, and the other requires again zu, as :

He was made an officer, er wurde zum Offizier gemacht.

Mr. N. was appointed captain, er wurde zum Hauptmann ernannt (or ist zum Hauptmann ernannt worden).

Note. — The verbs halten, "to consider," "to think," erklären, "to declare," require in German the preposition für, as:

He was declared innocent, er wurde für unschuldig erklärt.

I considered everything lost, ich hielt alles für verloren.

Schelten, schimpfen, "to call names," nennen, heißen, "to call," which four verbs govern in the active two accusatives in German, require two nominatives in the passive, as:

He called him an honest man, er nannte ihn einen ehrlichen Mann.

He was called an honest man, er wurde ein ehrlicher Mann genannt.

---

42. The Wise Judge.

A rich but very stingy man had once lost a large sum of money, which was sewed up [1] in a leather [2]-bag. As quickly as possible he made his loss known through the papers, [3] and offered [4] the finder a reward of one hundred dollars. Soon after a man came to him saying: "Sir, I have read your notice [5] in the paper, and I think I have found your money." The rich man looked pleased as he took his cherished [6] money, which he at one time thought was lost. [7]

He then counted the money carefully, thinking at the same time how he could possibly defraud the honest man. Finally he said to him: "My good man, there were eight hundred dollars in this bag, but I find only seven hundred in it. You have very likely taken out one hundred dollars as your promised [8] reward." The honest man assured the rich man that he had not opened the bag, and that he brought it as he had found it.

They at last came to court. They both insisted [9] upon their former statements, [10] but the wise judge soon found a way [11] out of this difficulty [12]; he gave the following decision [13]: "You," he said, speaking to the rich man, "have lost a bag with eight hundred dollars in it, and this man has found a bag with seven hundred dollars, which, therefore, cannot be the one you have lost. You," speaking to the honest finder, "will keep the bag containing [14] seven hundred dollars until the man comes who has lost that sum ; and you, my good sir," he said to the other one, "you must wait patiently until the person comes who has found your eight hundred dollars."

[1] to sew up in, einnähen in (acc.). [2] lebern. [3] Zeitung (f., pl. –en). [4] bieten (dat.), versprechen (dat.). [5] Anzeige (f., pl. –en). [6] geschätzt. [7] to think to be lost, für verloren halten. [8] versprochen (adj.). [9] to insist upon, bestehen auf (dat.). [10] Aussage (f., pl. –n, use sing.). [11] Ausweg (m., pl. –e). [12] Schwierigkeit (f., pl. –en). [13] Entscheidung (f.), Ausspruch (m., pl. –sprüche). [14] to contain, enthalten.

43. The Wolf and the Dog.

One day a wolf met a dog in [1] the field. "How do you do [2] nephew," said the wolf, "I am glad to see you with all my heart. [3] Why, dear nephew, how fat you are! What is the cause of that [4]? I am half-starved [5] ; I am so lean [6] that you can almost see my ribs, and can count my bones."

"Why, uncle," said the dog, "I serve [7] a good master. I guard [8] his house from [8] thieves, and he gives me a comfortable [9] kennel, [10] and plenty to eat. He always gives me the best meat, nice bones and fresh milk."

"Is that it [11] ?" said the wolf. "Then I should also like to serve such a master. Will you not try to see if you can do something for me?"

"I will gladly do that," replied the dog; "come with me, and I doubt not in the least [12] that [13] I can help [14] you to a good place."

The wolf went with him, and as they were going along he discovered a bare [15] spot [16] on the neck of the dog. "Why, nephew," said the wolf then, "what do I see here? Your neck is quite bare." "Yes, uncle, that is only the mark [17] of the chain my master puts on [18] me in the day-time, so that I may not bite [19] his friends." "Indeed!" said the wolf, "if that is the case, you may keep your kind master, and your meat and nice bones, and your chain too.²⁰ I would rather go when and where²¹ I please,²² and be lean, than be a slave all my life for the sake of²³ nice food²⁴." With these words he sprang into the woods, and did not even²⁵ say good-bye²⁶ to his nephew.

¹ auf. ² to do, ſich befinden (the second person of singular is always used in fables). ³ with all my heart, von ganzem Herzen. ⁴ wie geht das zu. ⁵ verhungert. ⁶ mager, dürre. ⁷ dienen (dat.). ⁸ to guard from, bewachen vor. ⁹ bequem, behaglich. ¹⁰ Hütte (f., pl. –n), Hundehütte. ¹¹ iſt es das. ¹² im Geringſten. ¹³ that, daß. ¹⁴ helfen (dat.). ¹⁵ kahl. ¹⁶ Fleck (m., pl. –e), Stelle (f., pl. –n). ¹⁷ Zeichen (n.). ¹⁸ to put on, anlegen (dat.). ¹⁹ I may not bite = I do not bite. ²⁰ dazu. ²¹ wohin. ²² gefallen. ²³ for the sake of, um ... willen (prep., gen.); for God's sake, um Gottes willen. ²⁴ Futter (n.). ²⁵ not even, nicht einmal, nicht ſo viel als. ²⁶ Lebewohl.

44. The Old Horse's Appeal.¹

Once upon a time, many years ago, there lived a king,² who was a very just man and who liked his subjects. He wished justice to be done to all his people.³ Therefore he had a bell hung up, so that every one, who had a complaint to make,⁴ could ring⁵ it. In such a case he called⁶ a council⁷ of wise men together⁶ to decide⁸ the matter.

The lower part of the bell-rope⁹ was worn off¹⁰ from long use, and to lengthen¹¹ it somebody had fastened to it¹² a piece of vine¹³ from a bush near by. It once happened that a knight had a noble horse, which had served him for many a year; but this horse had grown old and useless, and the knight had turned¹⁴ him into a field to take care of himself.¹⁵ This old horse wandered about¹⁶ from place to place, and one day, having strayed¹⁷ to the spot where this bell was hanging, he began biting at¹⁸ the vine, and the bell rang out¹⁹ loud. The council came together, and when they found that it was a half-starved horse asking for justice,²⁰ they investigated the case, and decided that the knight, the owner of the poor old horse, should feed and care for him. And the king added²¹ a heavy fine,²² if the knight did not do his duty to²³ the old animal.

¹ Klage (f., pl. –n), Anklage (f.), Berufung (f., pl. -en). ² many years
ago there once lived a king (" there,,' see the end of notes). ³ wished
that justice, etc. = wünschte, daß seinem ganzen Volk Gerechtigkeit gethan
werde, or widerfahren sollte. ⁴ to make a complaint, Klage führen.
⁵ läuten. ⁶ to call together, zusammenrufen. ⁷ Rat (m., pl. Räte). ⁸ entscheiden. ⁹ Glockenstrang (m., pl. -stränge). ¹⁰ to wear off, abnutzen.
¹¹ befestigen an, or binden an. ¹² Ranke (f., pl. –n). ¹³ verlängern. ¹⁴ treiben. ¹⁵ to take care of one's self, für sich selbst zu sorgen. ¹⁶ to wander
about, herumschweifen. ¹⁷ sich verirren. ¹⁸ an (dat.). ¹⁹ to ring out, er-
klingen, ertönen. ²⁰ to ask for justice, um Gerechtigkeit nachsuchen. ²¹ hinzufügen. ²² schwere Strafe (f.). ²³ gegen.

Remarks.

"It is, there is, there are, there was, there were," are in German: es ist, es sind, es war, es waren; es giebt, es gab. Es ist,
es sind, etc., express a definite existence, and a small, distinct
place is usually mentioned, as:

1. Es ist keine Milch in dem Kruge.
   There is no milk in the pitcher.

2. Es ist eine Maus in der Falle.
   There is a mouse in the trap.

When something in general is expressed, and not a small,
definite place is spoken of, es giebt or es gab is to be used, as:

1. Es giebt schöne Vögel in Afrika.
   There are beautiful birds in Africa.

2. Es giebt keine Löwen in Amerika.
   There are no lions in America.

3. Es giebt viele reiche Kaufleute in Boston.
   There are many rich merchants in Boston.

At times either may be used, we may say with equal propriety, as:

Es sind or es giebt viele reiche Kaufleute in Boston.

When es in es ist, es sind etc., is a mere expletive, it is not
expressed when it does not begin the sentence, as:

1. Es ist heute ein schöner Tag.
It is a fine day to-day.
Ist heute ein schöner Tag?

3. Es sind viele Vögel in dem Garten.
There are many birds in the garden.
Sind viele Vögel auf diesem Baum?
Are there many birds in this tree?

4. Es ist kalt heute.
It is cold to-day.
Ist es kalt heute?

With es giebt, es gab, etc., es must always be used, as:

1. Es giebt dieses Jahr viele Äpfel.
There are many apples this year.
Giebt es dieses Jahr viele Äpfel?
Are there many apples this year?

Es giebt, es gab, always remain in the singular, and the subject in English becomes the object in the accusative case in German, as:

Es giebt einen Mann.
There is a man.

---

45. The Cunning Elephant.

There was once in India a rich Englishman. He lived with his family in the country in a charming villa, surrounded by high shade-trees. The doors of the dining-hall[1] opened[2] into a large garden, and, as fresh air is the greatest necessity[3] in so hot a country, these doors usually stood wide open. This English gentleman owned a young elephant, which was very tame, and of which his children were very fond. Whenever[4] the family sat at the table, this elephant would come[5] into the hall through an open door, place[6] himself behind the chairs of the children and help[7] himself to food from their plates. That pleased the children, and they gave him all he wanted.[8]

One day this gentleman had guests from the city, among whom was a young cadet who sat with the children. As usual, the elephant came in from the garden at dinner-time, and wanted to help himself from the plate of the cadet, as well as from those of the children. But the cadet, not being used to[9] such familiarities, stuck[10] his fork into the elephant's trunk. The elephant, drawing back[11] his trunk, went out of the same door through which he had come in; but the children were very sorry[12] that their pet[13] had been hurt.[14]

Suddenly the elephant came back into the hall, holding in his trunk a shrub which he had torn out[15] of the ground[16] by[17] its roots. This shrub had grown on an ant-hill, and shrub, roots and earth were covered all over[18] with these little insects, the bite of which is so very painful, as some of you perhaps know to your sorrow.[19] The elephant stepped[20] behind his enemy and shook the earth, and consequently the ants, over the head of the cadet. In a very brief space of time[21] the ants crept over his neck and face, and bit him so[22] that, without doubt, he would have cried out[23] aloud had he not been ashamed[24] to do so in company; but, as it was,[25] he had to take[26] in silence the joke which the animal played upon[27] him, for it paid him in the same coin.[28]

[1] Speifefaal (m., pl. -fäle). [2] führen. [3] Bedürfnis (n., pl. -ffe). [4] jedes-mal, wenn. [5] would (was accustomed to) come. [6] fich ftellen. [7] to help one's self, nehmen, zugreifen, fich zulangen. [8] fo viel er wollte. [9] to be used to, gewohnt fein an. [10] ftechen mit. [11] to draw back, zurückziehen. [12] to be sorry, leid thun, es thut mir leid. [13] Liebling (m., pl. -e). [14] that one had hurt, to hurt, wehe thun. [15] to tear out, reißen. [16] Boden (m.). [17] mit. [18] über und über. [19] zu Ihrem Leid. [20] treten. [21] in a very brief space of time, in einer fehr kurzen Zeit. [22] fo. [23] to cry out, fchreien. [24] fich fchämen. [25] but as it was, fo aber. [26] to have to take, hinnehmen müffen. [27] to play upon, treiben mit. [28] in the same coin, mit gleicher Münze.

46. Boys Decide a Case in Law.[1]

A man once fell from the steep bank of a river into the water, and would have been drowned[2] had not somebody, who was near,[3] heard his cry[4] and hastened to his assistance.[5] His deliverer[6] held[7] a pole out to[7] him, and he helped[8] himself out[8] with it, knocking out[9] one of his eyes, however, in doing so.[10] Therefore he appeared in court the next day, brought[11] an action against[11] his deliverer, and claimed[12] damages[13] for his lost eye. The judge did not know what to do in the case, and postponed[14] the decision until[14] the next session. But the third session came, and still the judge was not settled[15] in his mind.[15]

Out of humor,[16] he mounted his horse,[17] and rode slowly and thoughtfully towards the city where the court was held. On his way[18] he came upon[19] three shepherd-boys, who were sitting on a heap of stones,[20] and who seemed to be transacting[21] some business of importance. "What are you doing there, children?" he asked them. "We are playing court," was the answer. "Well, what case have[22] you on[22]?" he asked farther. "We are holding court about[23] the man who fell into the river," they answered. Then he held in[24] his horse to wait for the decision.[25]

The boys did not recognize him, because he was wrapped[26] in his cloak, and they did not let[27] themselves be disturbed.[27] It was then decided[28] by them that the man rescued[29] should be thrown into the river again at[30] the same place; if he then could save himself, he should receive damages ; if not, he should lose his case.

Before the judge rode on,[31] he put[32] his hand into his pocket, and threw[33] the boys a piece of money. In court he decided as the shepherd-boys had done. The rascal really could not save himself, and thus[34] the other one gained the law-suit.[35]

---

[1] Rechtsfall (m., pl. -fälle). [2] to be drowned, ertrinken. [3] to be near, in der Nähe sein. [4] Geschrei (n.). [5] to hasten to his assistance, ihm zu Hilfe eilen. [6] Erretter (m.). [7] to hold out to, entgegen halten (dat.). [8] to help one's self out, sich heraushelfen. [9] to knock out, ausstoßen. [10] in doing so, dabei. [11] to bring an action against = to sue, verklagen. [12] verlangen. [13] Ersatz (m.). [14] to postpone until, verschieben auf. [15] to

be settled in one's mind, mit fidj einig fein. [16] mißlaunig. [17] to mount
the horse, auffteigen, or auf das Pferd fteigen. [18] unterwegs. [19] to come
upon, treffen. [20] Steinhaufen (m.). [21] verhandeln. [22] to have on, vorhaben. [23] über. [24] to hold in, anhalten. [25] Urteil (n., pl. –e). [26] hüllen
in. [27] to let one's self be disturbed, fidj ftören laffen. [28] to be decided,
für redjt erfennen. [29] the man rescued = the rescued man. [30] an.
[31] weiter. [32] greifen. [33] zuwerfen (dat.). [34] fo, auf diefe Weife. [35] Pro-
zeß' (m., pl. –e).

47. The Dying Father.

A father left behind two heirs.
His Christopher was clever,[1] George was dull and weak.
Ere fast approaching [2] death dissolved [3] his cares,
With grief [4] on Christopher he looked, then thus did speak :
" My son, a melancholy thought torments my mind.
Thou 'st talent, how wilt thou in future fare [5]?
Now hear me : In my chest [6] thou 'lt find
A little box [7] of jewels rare ;
They shall be thine.   Take all, my son,
And give not to thy brother one ! "
The son, alarmed,[8] began to grieve.
"Ah ! father," he replied, " if I so much receive,
How will my brother George get on [9]? "
" He ? " cried the father.   " O, my son,
No anxious care I feel [10] for George's sake,[10]
His dullness will his fortune make."

Ch. F. Gellert.

[1] gewandt, gefdjidt. [2] herannahend. [3] beendigen. [4] mit Betrübnis,
betrübt. [5] ergehen (dat.). [6] Rifte (f., pl. –n). [7] Schachtel (f., pl. –n). [8] er-
fdjroden. [9] fortfommen. [10] to feel for . . . sake, Sorge haben um.

48. The Bee and the Gardener's Daughter.

Once a little bee there flew
Busily [1] about,[2] and drew [3]
Sweets from every blooming flower.

"Little bee," the maiden cried,
Who was busy there at work,[4]
"Oft therein doth poison lurk,[5]
And thou sipp'st[6] from every flower."
"Yes," said the bee, "the sweets I sup,[7]
But leave the poison in the cup[8]."

G. L. Gleim.

[1] emſig. [2] umher, hin und her. [3] ſaugen. [4] bei der Arbeit. [5] to lurk, verſteckt liegen, ſein. [6] einſaugen. [7] ſchlürfen. [8] Kelch (m., pl. -e), calyx.

---

48. Scene from Nephew as Uncle.

BY SCHILLER.

Sophia de Dorsigny.   *De Lormeuil.*

Sophia. — Then you[1] will be at[2] the wedding[3] also?

Lormeuil. — Yes, Miss Dorsigny. This marriage[5] does not seem to displease[4] you.

Soph. — It has the approbation of my father.

Lorm. — Well; but what fathers arrange[6] has not, therefore, always the daughter's consent.

Soph. — Oh, what matters[7] this marriage! It has been partly my own arranging.

Lorm. — How so, Miss Dorsigny?

Soph. — My father was so good as to consult[8] my inclination.[9]

Lorm. — Then you love the young man who is proposed[10] for your husband?

Soph. — I do not conceal it.

Lorm. — How? And do not yet know him?

Soph. — I was brought up[11] with him.

Lorm. — You were brought up with young Lormeuil?

Soph. — With Mr. de Lormeuil ... No!

Lorm. — But he is your intended[12] bridegroom.

Soph. — Yes, was at first.

Lorm. — How, at first?

Soph. — I see that you do not yet know, sir.

Lorm. — I know nothing.   Not the least thing [13] do I know.

Soph. — He is dead.

Lorm. — Who is dead?

Soph. — Young Mr. de Lormeuil.

Lorm. — Really?

Soph. — Most certainly.[14]

Lorm. — Who has told you that he is dead?

Soph. — My father.

Lorm. — Not so,[15] Miss Dorsigny.   That cannot be, that is impossible.

Soph. — With your permission, it is!   My father, who just comes from Toulon, must know better than you, I think.   This young nobleman had a quarrel [16] at a ball, he fought,[17] and received three sword wounds [18] through his body.

Lorm. — That is dangerous.

Soph. — Yes, indeed!   He died from [19] it.

Lorm. — You are pleased [20] to joke with me, my lady.   No one can give you a better account [21] of Mr. de Lormeuil than I.

Soph. — Than you!   That would be strange [22] though.[23]

Lorm. — Yes, Miss Dorsigny, than I!   For, to speak out [24] at once, I myself am this de Lormeuil, and I am not dead, so far [25] as I know.

Soph. — You are Mr. de Lormeuil?

Lorm. — Well, for whom else did you take me?

Soph. — For a friend of my father's, whom he has invited to my wedding.

Lorm. — You still celebrate [26] a wedding then, notwithstanding I am dead?

Soph. — Yes, certainly!

Lorm. — And with whom then, may I ask [27]?

Soph. — With my cousin Dorsigny.

Lorm. — But your father also would have a word to speak on the subject,[28] I suppose [29]?

Soph. — That he has, of course!   Indeed, he has given his consent.

Lorm. — When did he give it?

Soph. — Just now — a few moments before your arrival.

Lorm. — But I came at the same time with him.

Soph. — Not so, sir! My father was here before you.

Lorm. (*grasping his head*[30]) — I am giddy[31]! Everything turns[32] before my eyes! Every word that you say, astonishes[33] me! All respect to your words,[34] Miss Dorsigny; but there must be a mystery under this[35] which I cannot fathom.[36]

Soph. — How, sir? Have you really spoken in earnest?

Lorm. — In the greatest[37] earnestness.[38]

Soph. — You are really Mr. de Lormeuil? My God! what have I done! How will my imprudence[39]——

Lorm. — Do not let it trouble[40] you, Miss Dorsigny. Your affection for your cousin is a circumstance one[41] had better learn[42] before than after marriage.

Soph. — But I cannot comprehend——

Lorm. — I will go in quest of[43] Mr. de Dorsigny; perhaps he can explain[44] this riddle.[45] But be it explained as it may,[46] Miss Dorsigny, you will be satisfied with me, I hope. (*Exit.*[47])

Soph. — He appears like a very nice gentleman — and if they do not compel[48] me to marry[49] him, I shall be very glad that he is not stabbed.[50]

---

[1] alfo. [2] bei, auf. [3] Hochzeit (f., pl. –en). [4] mißfallen (dat.). [5] Heirat (f.). [6] anordnen. [7] betreffen. [8] to consult, um Rat fragen. [9] Neigung (f., pl. –en). [10] vorschlagen, bestimmen. [11] to bring up, erziehen. [12] bestimmt (adj.). [13] the least thing, Geringste (n.). [14] ganz gewiß. [15] Nicht doch. [16] Streit (m.). [17] sich schlagen. [18] Schwertwunde (f.), Degenstich (m., pl. –e). [19] to die from, sterben an. [20] you are pleased, es beliebt Ihnen. [21] Auskunft (f., pl. –en). [22] sonderbar, wunderlich. [23] doch. [24] to speak out, heraussagen. [25] weit. [26] halten. [27] if I may ask, dürfen. [28] bei der Sache, zu der Sache. [29] doch. [30] an den Kopf faffend. [31] schwindelig. [32] sich drehen. [33] in Erstaunen setzen. [34] all respect to your words, Ihre Worte in Ehren. [35] there is under this, hierunter steckt. [36] ergründen. [37] höchst. [38] Ernst (m.). [39] Unbesonnenheit (f.). [40] beunruhigen. [41] man. [42] erfahren. [43] to go in quest of, auffuchen. [44] löfen. [45] Rätfel (n.). [46] but be it explained as it may, aber wie es sich auch immer auflösen mag. [47] ab. [48] zwingen. [49] heiraten. [50] to stab, erstechen.

49. Extracts[1] from "Minna von Barnhelm."

BY G. E. LESSING.

Major von Tellheim.   Just, his servant.

Tellheim — Art thou there[3]?

Just (wiping his eyes) — Yes.

Tell. — Thou hast been crying.

Just — I have been writing out my bill in the kitchen, and the kitchen is full of smoke.[4] Here it is, sir.

Tell. — Give it to me.

Just — Have compassion[5] on me, sir. I know well that people have none for you, but ——

Tell. — What do you want?

Just — I should have[6] sooner[7] expected[8] my death than my discharge.[9]

Tell. — I have no longer[10] any need[19] of thy services. I must learn to make shift without[11] a servant. (*Opens the bill and reads.*) 'What the major owes[12] me : Three and a half month's wages,[13] 6 dollars a month, makes 21 dollars. Since the first of this month laid out[14] for trifles 1 dollar, 7 groschen, 9 pfennigs.' Good! and it is but right[15] I should pay up the full month.

Just — The other side, Major.

Tell. — More still? (*Reads.*) 'What I owe the major : Paid the army-surgeon for me 25 dollars; for waiting[16] and nursing[17] during my illness, 39 dollars. To my plundered[18] and burned-out[19] father advanced,[20] at my request, without taking into account[21] the two horses of which he made him a present,[22] 50 dollars; altogether, 114 dollars. The before-named[23] 22 doll., 7 gr., 9 pf. deducted, remain due[24] to the major 91 dollars, 16 groschens, 3 pfennings.' — Fellow, art thou mad?

Just — I have no doubt I cost you a great deal more, but it would be waste of ink[25] to write it down. I cannot pay you, and if you, moreover, take my livery,[26] which I have also not earned, I would rather[27] you had let me die in the hospital.

Tell.— What dost thou take me for ? Thou owest me nothing, and I recommend[28] thee to one of my acquaintances with whom thou wilt fare better[29] than with me.

Just— I owe you nothing, and yet you will send me away !

Tell.— Because I will owe thee nothing.

·*Just* — For that reason[30] only ? For that ?— As surely[31] as I am in your debt, as surely as you cannot be in mine, so surely you ought not now to turn[32] me away.[32] Do as you please,[33] Major, I will remain with[34] you ; I must remain with you.

[1] Auszug (m., pl. -züge). [2] da. [3] wischen. [4] Rauch (m.). [5] to have compassion on, Barmherzigkeit haben mit. [6] I should have = I had (use subj. mode). [7] eher. [8] vermuten. [9] Abschied (m., pl. -e). [10] no longer any need, kein weiterer Gebrauch. [11] I must learn to make shift without, ich muß ... entbehren lernen, or ich muß mich ohne ... behelfen lernen. [12] schulden (dat.). [13] Sold (m., *military wages*). [14] auslegen. [15] but right, nicht mehr als recht, billig. [16] Wartung (f.). [17] Pflege (f.). [18] geplündert. [19] abgebrannt. [20] ausgelegt, vorgeschossen. [21] to take into account, rechnen, in Rechnung ziehen. [22] of which he ... a present = which he presented to him = schenken (dat.). [23] die obengenannten 22 Dollars, etc., abgezogen. [24] bleibe ich schuldig. [25] lost ink (f.). [26] Livree (f.), Anzug (m., pl. -züge). [27] ich wollte lieber. [28] empfehlen (dat.). [29] to fare well, gut haben, ich habe es gut, or gut gehen, es geht mir wohl, es geht mir gut. [30] for that reason, darum, deswegen. [31] gewiß. [32] to turn away, entlassen, verabschieden. [33] do as you please = do what you will. [34] bei.

50.

Minna v. Barnhelm. Francisca, her servant. *Landlord. Just.*

(Enter[1] *Landlord* and *Just.*)

Landl. — I have brought[2] him with the greatest trouble.

Franc. — A strange face. I don't know him.

Minna— My friend, are you with[3] Major von Tellheim ?

Just — Yes.

Minna — Where is your master ?

Just — Not here.

Minna — But you know where to find him ?

Just — Yes.

Minna — Will you not fetch⁴ him directly?

Just — No.

Minna — You would oblige⁵ me by doing so.⁶

Just — Eh!

Minna — And render⁷ your master a service.

Just — Perhaps not exactly.

Minna — Why do you suppose that?

Just — You, of course, are the strange family who sent their compliments this morning?

Minna — Yes.

Just — Then I am right, you see.

Minna — Does your master know my name?

Just — No, but he as much dislikes the over-polite ladies, as the over-rude⁸ landlords.

Landl. — He means that for me as well, I suppose⁹?

Just — Yes.

Landl. — Well, but don't make¹⁰ the lady suffer for it,¹⁰ and fetch him here directly.

Minna (to *Franc.*) — Francisca, give him something ——

Franc. (*putting money into Just's hand*) — We don't require¹¹ your services without paying.

Just — Nor I your money without service.

Franc. — One for the other.

Just — I cannot; my master has ordered me to remove¹² his things.¹³ I am going to do so now, and I beg you will hinder me no longer. When I have done¹⁴ I will tell him certainly that he can come here. He is close by,¹⁵ at¹⁶ the coffee-house, and if he finds nothing better to do, he will most likely come. (*Is going.*)

Franc. — Well, but wait, the lady is the major's sister ——

Minna — Yes, yes, his sister.

Just — I know better; the major has no sister. He sent me twice in six months to his family in Courland.¹⁷ — To be sure,¹⁸ there are several sorts¹⁹ of sisters ——

Franc. — Impudent fellow²⁰!

Just — Must one not be so[21] when people won't let him alone? (*Exit.*)

Franc. — That man is a scoundrel !

[1] eintreten. [2] Use pres. tense. [3] bei. [4] holen. [5] verbinden (acc.), einen Gefallen thun (dat.). [6] by doing so, damit. [7] erzeigen (dat.), erweisen (dat.). [8] over-rude, allzu grob. [9] I suppose, wohl. [10] to make suffer for it, es entgelten lassen. [11] verlangen. [12] wegschaffen, entfernen. [13] Sache (f., pl. -n). [14] when I have done = when I am ready. [15] nebenan. [16] auf. [17] Curland, Kurland (was formerly a dukedom, belongs since 1795 to the Russian empire). [18] zwar. [19] mancherlei. [20] Unverschämter. [21] es.

---

51. Brief Extract from "A Christmas Carol."

BY CHARLES DICKENS.

MARLEY'S GHOST.

Marley was dead, to begin with.[1] There is no doubt whatever[2] about that. The register[3] of his burial[3] was signed by the clergyman, the clerk,[4] the undertaker, and the chief mourner.[5] Scrooge signed it, and Scrooge's name was good upon 'change[6] for anything[7] he chose to put his hand to.[7] Old Marley was as dead as a door-nail.

Mind[8] ! I don't mean to say that I know, of my own knowledge[9] what there is particularly dead about[10] a door-nail. I might have been inclined[11] myself to regard[12] a coffin-nail as[12] the deadest piece of ironmongery in the trade. But the wisdom of our ancestors is in the simile, and my unhallowed hands shall not disturb it, or the country 's done[13] for. You will, therefore, permit me to repeat emphatically that Marley was as dead as a door-nail.

Scrooge knew he was dead? Of course he did. How could it be otherwise? Scrooge and he were partners[14] for I don't know how many years. Scrooge was his sole executor, his sole administrator, his sole assign,[15] his sole residuary legatee, his sole friend and his sole mourner. And even Scrooge was not so dreadfully cut up [16] by the sad event, but that [17] he was an excellent man of business on the very day [18] of the funeral, and solemnized it with an undoubted bargain.[19]

The mention of Marley's funeral brings me back to the point I started [20] from. There is no doubt that Marley was dead. This must be distinctly [21] understood,[22] or nothing wonderful can come of the story [23] I am going to relate. If we were not perfectly convinced that Hamlet's father died before the play began, there would be nothing more remarkable in his taking a stroll [24] at night, in an easterly wind upon his own ramparts, than there would be in any other middle-aged gentleman [25] rashly turning [26] out after dark [27] in a breezy spot — say St. Paul's church-yard for instance — literally [28] to astonish [29] his son's weak mind.[30]

Scrooge never painted out [31] Old Marley's name. There it stood, years afterwards, above the warehouse [32] door : " Scrooge and Marley." The firm [33] was known as Scrooge and Marley. Sometimes people, new to the business,[34] called Scrooge Scrooge, and sometimes Marley; but he answered to [35] both names ; it was all the same [36] to [37] him.

[1] to begin with = in order to begin with that. [2] burdjauß. [3] Die Urkunde über seine Beſtattung, or Begräbnißſchein. [4] Schreiber, Küſter. [5] der vornehmſte (Trauernde or) Leidtragende. [6] 'Change = Exchange, Börſe (f., pl. -en). [7] for anything . . . his hand to = for whatever he chose to sign it (his name), wofür er ihn nur immer unterſchreiben wollte. [8] mark, but mark well. [9] of my own, etc. = aus meiner eigenen Kenntniß, or Erfahrung (f., pl. -en). [10] an (dat.). [11] to be inclined, geneigt ſein. [12] to regard as, halten für (acc.). [13] to be done for, es iſt geſchehen um, or iſt verloren, zu Grunde gerichtet. [14] Geſchäfts=Teilhaber, or Genoſſen, or in Kompagnie. [15] Bevollmächtigte (used as a noun, decl. like an adj.). [16] to be cut up, gerührt ſein. [17] but that = that he not. [18] on the very day . . . itself, or, even on the day. [19] Gewinn (m., pl. -e). [20] to start from, ausgehen. [21] unbedingt, beſtimmt. [22] to be understood, als Wahrheit angeſehen werden. [23] can come of the story = can be in the story. [24] in his taking a stroll = that he took a stroll ("in his taking," see remarks at the end of these notes). [25] middle-aged gentleman, ein Herr in or von mittleren Jahren. [26] to turn out, hinausgehen. [27] nach

Sonnenuntergang (m., pl. –gänge). [28] literally = only, or, in fact only, nur. [29] in Erstaunen setzen. [30] weak mind = weak-minded, schwachsinnig (adj.). [31] ausstreichen. [32] Lager (n.), Waarenlager (n.), Niederlage (f., pl. –n). [33] Firma (f.). [34] new to the business = who were not acquainted with the business. [35] to answer to, antworten auf, or hören auf. [36] all the same, ganz gleich. [37] ihm (dat.).

Additional Remarks on the Translation of the English Present Participle.

a) When in English the present participle is preceded by a possessive adjective, with or without a preposition, the German must be expressed by a subordinate clause with a conjunction, and the possessive adjective is changed into the personal pronoun and becomes the subject.

The following will help in fixing the German conjunctions to be used in such cases:

"Of, at, *or* in," daß; "without," ohne daß; "before," ehe; "against," dagegen, daß; "by," dadurch, daß; "on *or* upon," darauf, daß.

1. His taking a walk every morning is the physician's desire.
   Daß er jeden Morgen einen Spaziergang macht, ist des Arztes Wunsch.

2. We heard of his buying a horse.
   Wir hörten, daß (or davon, daß) er ein Pferd kaufen will.

3. They noticed our looking at them.
   Sie bemerkten, daß wir sie ansahen.

4. He went away without his bidding us farewell.
   Er ging fort, ohne daß er uns Lebewohl sagte.

5. He went to the store before his coming home.
   Er ging in den Laden, ehe er nach Hause kam.

6. The father had nothing against their going into the country.
   Der Vater hatte nichts dagegen, daß sie auf das Land gingen.

7. He insisted upon our coming back.
   Er bestand darauf, daß wir zurückkommen sollten.

8. He caught the thief by (his) jumping over the wall.

Er fing ben Dieb baburdh, baß er über bie Mauer fprang.

b) When in English a noun in the genitive is preceded by a possessive adjective, and is then followed by a present participle, a subordinate clause also must be formed, the noun in the genitive becoming the subject, as :

1. The pupil went out without his teacher's seeing it.

Der Schüler ging hinaus, ohne baß fein Lehrer es fah.

2. He wished to write his exercise before his brother's coming home.

Er wollte feine Aufgabe fchreiben, ehe fein Bruder nach Haufe fam.

Remarks on the Infinitive.

A. THE INFINITIVE WITH zu.

Excepting in the cases already given, in which the infinitive with zu, "to," is used in German to translate the English present participle, the two languages correspond closely in their use of it, as :

1. Have you a desire to go to the theater?

Haben Sie Luft, ins Theater zu gehen?

2. I am anxious to learn who it is.

Ich bin begierig zu erfahren, wer es ift.

3. It is easy to learn this poem.

Es ift leicht, biefes Gebicht zu lernen, *or* biefes Gebicht ift leicht zu lernen.

4. I have much to do.

Ich habe biel zu thun.

5. He has to tell you something, *or*, he has something to tell you.

Er hat Ihnen etwas zu fagen.

6. He feared to be (come) too late.

Er fürchtete zu fpät zu fommen.   **Etc.**

B. Infinitive without zu.

(Here again the two languages correspond very closely.)

I. The infinitive without zu is used after the auxiliaries of mode: können, wollen, sollen, mögen, müssen, dürfen.

II. After the following verbs: sehen, hören, fühlen, heißen ("to bid"), machen, lassen, lernen, lehren and helfen, as:

1. She can speak English.
   Sie kann Englisch sprechen.

2. He does not want to (will not) go to school.
   Er will nicht in die Schule gehen.

3. We must stay at home.
   Wir müssen zu Hause bleiben.   Etc.

4. I saw him go (going) home.
   Ich sah ihn nach Hause gehen.

5. I heard the birds sing (singing).
   Ich hörte die Vögel singen.

6. This boy learns to paint.
   Dieser Knabe lernt malen.

7. He taught me to row.
   Er lehrte mich rudern.   Etc.

All the verbs mentioned above, with the exception of fühlen and lehren, and sometimes lernen and hören, have the peculiarity that in the compound past tenses they use the infinitive instead of the past participle when another infinitive precedes them, as:

1. He has not been able to come.
   Er hat nicht kommen können (*not* gekonnt).

2. They have not wished (did not want) to sing.
   Sie haben nicht singen wollen (*not* gewollt), etc.

3. I have seen her go away.
   Ich habe sie weggehen sehen (*not* gesehen).

4. I have heard her sing.
Ich habe sie singen hören.

5. Where have you learned (did you learn) to speak English.
Wo haben Sie englisch sprechen lernen (*or* gelernt).   Etc.

III. The infinitive without zu is further used in some particular expressions with the following verbs:

Bleiben, "to remain," liegen bleiben, sitzen bleiben, stehen
    bleiben.

Legen, "to lay," schlafen legen.

Gehen, "to go;" reiten, "to ride (on horseback);" fahren,
"to ride in a carriage;" spazieren gehen, "to go walking;" spazieren reiten, "to take a ride;" spazieren fahren, "to take a
drive;" schlafen gehen, "to go to sleep;" betteln gehen, "to go
begging."

These words mentioned last always retain the past participle in the compound tenses, as:

1. Ich habe das Kind schlafen gelegt.
2. Das Messer ist unter dem Tische liegen geblieben.
3. Wir sind spazieren gegangen, geritten, gefahren.
4. Die Kinder sind schlafen gegangen.   Etc.

ALPHABETICAL INDEX.

118

INDEX.

ADVERTISEMENTS.

MODERN LANGUAGES.

Beginners' Book in French.

Illustrated with humorous pictures. By SOPHIE DORIOT. Square 12mo. Boards. 304 pages. Mailing Price, 90 cents; for introduction, 80 cents. **Part II.** — *Reading Lessons* (separate). 186 pages. Mailing Price, 55 cents; for introduction, 50 cents.

CHILDREN, for whom this book is designed, care nothing for the intrinsic meaning or value of words. In order to obtain satisfactory results in teaching them a foreign language, it is necessary to amuse them, awaken their enthusiasm, or appeal to their sympathy. In object-teaching, it requires teachers of exceptional ability or of special energy to experience and communicate a never-failing enthusiasm about the chair they are sitting on, or the table placed before them. On the other hand, the author has found that by giving children and other beginners subjects which they like, or which are calculated to excite their curiosity, they will, in order to conquer the point which is luring them, master words and expressions in a time and manner that cannot be secured by the best-arranged methods.

It is on this principle that the present book has been prepared. It is intended as a relief to teachers, aud a source of pleasure as well as instruction to young pupils. The pictures have been made as humorous as possible. They are exact illustrations of the text following them, having been drawn expressly to accompany it.

E. S. Joynes, *Prof. of Modern Languages, South Carolina College:* It makes the beginning of French so charming that all the children who see it will be crying to learn French. I have never seen any similar book so exquisitely conceived and so faithfully and beautifully executed. (*Feb.* 20, 1887.)

Le Francais, *Boston:* C'est bien là le livre que les maîtres devraient mettre entre les mains des *enfants américains* qui étudient notre langue. (*February,* 1887.)

Courrier des Etats Unis, *New York:* Son auteur . . . a parfaitement réussi. (*Feb.* 28, 1887.)

Beginners' Book in German.

Illustrated with humorous pictures. By SOPHIE DORIOT, author of *The Beginners' Book in French.* Square 12mo.   pages. Boards. Mailing Price,   cents; for introduction,   cents.

THIS follows the natural method for which Miss Doriot's *Beginners' Book in French* has been so much commended. The lessons are introduced with a humorous picture, followed by some corresponding verses from the child-literature of Germany. A conversation upon the subject, with the study of words and phrases, completes the lesson. Advantage is thus taken of the learner's tastes and inclinations, and even of the mischief-loving element of young America.

The Second Part contains *graded selections* for reading, which may be issued separately, as in the case of *The Beginners' Book in French.*

Spiers' New French-English Dictionary.

Compiled from the French Dictionaries of L'Académie, Bescherelle, Littré, etc., and the English Dictionaries of Johnson, Webster, Richardson, etc., and the technical works in both languages. By Dr. SPIERS, Agrégé de l'Université, Chevalier de la Légion d'Honneur, Officier de l'Instruction Publique. Twenty-ninth edition, entirely remodelled, revised, and largely increased by H. WITCOMB, successor to Dr. Spiers at the École des Ponts et Chaussées. Crown 8vo. Half morocco. 782 pages. Mailing Price, $4.85; for introduction, $4.50.

DR. SPIERS continued, so long as he lived, to collect materials for the improvement and the enlargement of his great work. These materials, supplemented where necessary, have now been incorporated by most competent hands, and this work, after forty years of success, is the newest exhaustive French Dictionary.

Spiers' English-French Dictionary.

Crown octavo. Half morocco. 910 pages. Mailing Price, $4.85; for introduction, $4.50.

THE plan of this work is similar to that of the French-English Dictionary.

M. Blanqui, *Membre de l'Institut:* Cet excellent ouvrage qui me semble digne au plus haut point de l'attention du monde savant. . . . C'est un travail tout a fait neuf, sérieux, approfondi, complet.

Modern French Readings.   ˧

Edited by WILLIAM I. KNAPP, Professor of Modern Languages in Yale College. 12mo. Cloth. 467 pages. Mailing Price, 90 cents ; Introduction, 80 cents.

THE selections have been made with reference to style and vocabulary, rather than to the history of the literature, so as to enable the reader to acquire experience in the popular, social, every-day terms and idioms that characterize the writings of the French to-day.   They embrace about a year's study.   ·

Tribune, *Chicago :* To familiarize the young with what may be called the French of the people, which now dominates the French of literature, the work of the accomplished professor of modern languages at Yale College cannot be too highly commended.

A Grammar of the Modern Spanish Language.

As now written and spoken in the Capital of Spain. By WILLIAM I. KNAPP, Professor in Yale College. 12mo. Cloth. 496 pages. Mailing Price, $1.65; Introduction, $1.50.

THIS book aims to set before the student, clearly and completely, yet concisely, the forms and usages of the present speech of the Castiles, and to fix them in the memory by a graded series of English-Spanish exercises.   The work is divided into two distinct parts, — a Grammar and a Drill-Book.

The inflected parts of speech are presented on a new, and, it is believed, a more judicious method, and the so-called irregular verbs are considerably reduced in number.   A few reading lessons are appended, with an appropriate vocabulary, for those who may not care to follow the exercises.

Schele De Vere, *Prof. of Modern Language, etc., University of Virginia :* After a careful, practical examination of your strikingly handsome edition of Professor Knapp's Grammar, I am convinced that it is by far the best work of its kind. Having myself published — many years ago — a Spanish Grammar, which in its day was successful, I ought to be no incompetent critic. I shall certainly use the book in this university. (*Dec.* 19, 1882.)

Modern Spanish Readings.

By WILLIAM I. KNAPP, Ph.D., Professor of Modern Languages, Yale College. 12mo. Cloth. 458 pages. Mailing Price, $1.65; Introduction, $1.50.

THE 200 pages of text represent the average modern style of composition in the newspaper article, the novel, the essay, history, and criticism.

George L. Andrews, *Prof. of Modern Languages, United States Military Academy, West Point, N.Y.:* Professor Knapp's Spanish Grammar and Modern Spanish Readings have been in use as text-books at the Military Academy for the last three years, and have been found very satisfactory. For any serious study of the Spanish Language by those whose vernacular is the English, I know of no other grammar that is nearly as good as that of Professor Knapp. (*March* 17, 1886.)

Spanish Idioms, with their English Equivalents,

Embracing nearly 10,000 phrases. By SARAH CARY BECKER and Señor FEDERICO MORA. 8vo. Cloth. 330 pages. Mailing Price, $2.00; for introduction, $1.80.

THIS is as nearly as possible a complete collection of Spanish idioms, or of Spanish phrases which, if literally translated, would fail to convey to foreign ears the sense in which they are understood by Spaniards. No approximately complete collection of these idioms has hitherto been published, either separately, or scattered through any more comprehensive work. The translations have been made with great care, and numerous errors in the readings found in Spanish-English dictionaries are here corrected. The idioms are arranged on a plan so simple that any phrase may be found with the utmost ease. Spanish literature and conversation fairly bristle with idioms, and this difficult feature of the language is here adequately dealt with for the first time.

J. F. Sagrario, *Sec'y of the Spanish Legation, Washington:* All the expressions are thoroughly idiomatic. They are *very* well translated. The book will be very useful, not only to beginners, but to the more advanced students.

An Alphabetical Table of German Prefixes and
Suffixes.

By WILLIAM COOK, Editor of *Otto's Grammar.* 4 pages of tough paper, 8 × 10 inches. Price, 5 cents.

THIS may be used either for reference or for regular lessons, in connection with any text-book.

German Lessons.

By W. C. COLLAR, A.M., Head Master of the Roxbury Latin School, Boston, and author of "The Beginner's Latin Book"; being "Eysenbach's Practical German Grammar" revised and largely rewritten, with Notes, Selections for Reading, and Vocabularies. 12mo. Cloth. xxiv + 360 pages. Mailing Price, $1.30; for introduction, $1.20.

EYSENBACH'S Grammar was the work of one who had a genius for teaching. It had a great merit of design, — it presented the language to the learner *right end foremost;* and a great merit in execution, — exercises wonderfully ingenious, copious, and varied. It was deficient in scientific spirit and method. This lack Mr. Collar was peculiarly fitted, as the *Beginner's Latin Book* showed, to supply. It is believed that the *German Lessons* harmonizes in a practical way the "natural" and the "scientific" methods.

It is **inductive,** as one proceeds instinctively and necessarily, when he learns a foreign language in a foreign country, — not rigidly inductive, but naturally and easily so.

It is **direct and simple,** presenting everything from its practical side, in such a way as to help most toward the *reading, writing,* and *speaking* of German with ease and accuracy.

It is **well-arranged,** because every topic is taken up in its right place, and the lessons are so ordered that the mastery of one is a stepping-stone to the mastery of the next; so that the pupil feels he is outflanking the difficulties.

It is **thorough,** particularly in the abundant, ingenious, and varied Exercises, in adhering to the principle that reading, writing, and speaking should go hand in hand, and in stating things with scholarly accuracy and finish.

And finally, it is **complete,** comprising Lessons, Precise Grammatical Principles, Choice Readings, Pertinent Notes, an Outline of Pronunciation, a Table of Contents, and an Index, — all in about 250 pages, besides the Vocabularies.

A. N. Van Daell, *Director of Instruction in the Modern Languages, Boston Public Schools:* Collar's Eysenbach's German Lessons is a decided advance on books of similar design. It is short and yet thorough in its treatment, easy and yet scholarly.

H. H. Boyesen, *Professor of German in Columbia College:* I like the Collar's Eysenbach's German Lessons better than any that have so far come to my notice. It embodies all that is of practical use in the so-called natural method, and the latest results of pedagogical experience.

O. Seidensticker, *Professor of German in the University of Pennsylvania:* The work has the very commendable feature of combining and very happily blending what is truly meritorious in the different systems. It leads by the directest way to a conversational use of German, and supplies the needful grammatical instruction.

W. R. Rosentengel, *Professor of German;* **S. A. Sterling,** *Instructor in German;* **J. E. Olson,** *Assistant Professor of Scandinavian Languages and German, University of Wisconsin:* After having examined Collar's Eysenbach's German Grammar, we recommend it for introduction into the University, and to the German teachers of the accredited high schools of this State.

W. H. Carruth, *Professor of German in the University of Kansas:* The arrangement under one series of lessons is highly desirable, and the English themes for translation into German seem to be the most human and probable that I have ever found in a grammar. The model idiomatic sentences at the beginning of each lesson are an excellent feature. . . . I think he has written the grammar I have been waiting for.

C. F. P. Bancroft, *Prin. of Phillips Academy, Andover, Mass.:* It is a serious, sensible, successful book. It has taken its place at once and by right at the front, among the few best German grammars and the fewer best first books in German.

Oscar Faulhaber, *Teacher of German, Phillips Acad., Exeter, N.H.:* An experienced teacher is bound to admire the pedagogic skill in its compilation. It has many advantages over other German grammars that will surely meet with speedy recognition by the profession.

Jas. A. Beatley, *Teacher of German, English High School, Boston, Mass.:* I have always said that Eysenbach's Grammar gave a pupil the chance to acquire the German language without filling his mind with lumber. I find the new edition an improvement on the old. (*Dec. 2, 1887.*)

Miss Kate W. Cushing, *Teacher of German, East Boston High School, Mass.:* Its method is terse, logical, and natural in the right sense of that much-abused word. The scholar's hand has left its mark on every page, and the very points which the author by experience knows a student of German is sure to need are concisely given in their proper place.

Wm. Fuller, *Teacher of German, High School, Lynn, Mass.:* The original work I have used in several classes with good results, and as far as my examination of it extends, the revision seems to enhance the value of what was already a useful textbook. (*Nov. 22, 1887.*)

M. Hinkel, *Prof. of German, Vassar College, N.Y.:* I am much pleased with it. It presents the essentials of grammar in a very clear, comprehensive manner, in the proper order, and without verbosity. The exercises also are eminently practical and to the point. Altogether I consider it an excellent book for beginners. (*Nov. 26, 1888.*)

J. B. Unthank, *Pres. of Wilmington College, Ohio:* I have as yet seen no book on the practical plan that I think equal to Collar's Eysenbach. (*Oct. 21, 1888.*)

Charles H. Jones, *Prin. of Oak Grove Seminary, Vassalboro, Me.:* It is a rare book. We are using it this term for the first time, and teacher and pupils are enthusiastic over it. (*Oct. 24, 1888.*)

English into German.

The English Exercises from Collar's Eysenbach's German Lessons. 12mo. Paper. ii + 51 pages. Mailing Price, 25 cents; for introduction, 20 cents.

IT is believed that this separate edition of the exercises for turning English into German will be a great convenience to teachers. After the exercises have been done once with the help of the special vocabularies and under the direction and criticism of the teacher, it will be found useful to review them again and again, sometimes orally, sometimes in writing, with all helps in the way of rules, special vocabularies, and model sentences removed. The pupil is thus left to depend entirely upon his previous study and faithful attention to his teacher's instruction.

German Exercises.

By J. FREDERICK STEIN, Instructor of German in the Boston High Schools. 12mo. Cloth. 118 pages. Mailing Price, 45 cents; for introduction, 40 cents.

THIS, the first and only book of its kind in German, is based on the reproduction plan, like Collar and Daniell's *Beginner's Latin Book*. It is designed as supplementary to any good grammar or "Lessons," and will answer as a first reader in German. The reproducing work may be commenced after a short study of the rudiments; and yet the book contains enough, in the second part, for pupils well advanced. It may be used with or without a grammar, since the notes are complete in themselves. Special pains have been taken to illustrate German construction. Though it is not a grammar, remarks are made on the principal grammatical rules, and while in most grammars such notes are scattered through a large volume, they are here given compactly and together. The design of the *German Exercises* is "to lead the pupil early into the spirit of the German by forming it."

John Tetlow, *Head Master of the Girls' High and Latin Schools, Boston; Author of Tetlow's Latin Lessons:* They furnish, in my judgment, very serviceable and very interesting material for the kind of composition and conversation which should accompany the beginner's work in German.

W. C. Collar, *Author of the Beginner's Latin Book, and Editor of Collar's Eysenbach's German Lessons:* I am happy to express my entire approval of the author's purpose and plan. I believe his method to be the most reasonable and interesting, as well as the most fruitful in good results.

BOOKS ON ENGLISH LITERATURE.

Allen	Reader's Guide to English History	$ .25
Arnold . . .	English Literature	1.50
Bancroft . .	A Method of English Composition	.50
Browne . .	Shakespere Versification	.25
Fulton & Trueblood:	Choice Readings	1.50
	Chart Illustrating Principles of Vocal Expression,	2.00
Genung . .	Practical Elements of Rhetoric	1.25
Gilmore . .	Outlines of the Art of Expression	.60
Ginn	Scott's Lady of the Lake . . . *Bds.,* .35; *Cloth,* .50	
	Scott's Tales of a Grandfather . *Bds.,* .40; *Cloth,* .50	
Gummere .	Handbook of Poetics	1.00
Hudson . .	Harvard Edition of Shakespeare : —	
	20 Vol. Edition. *Cloth, retail*	25.00
	10 Vol. Edition. *Cloth, retail*	20.00
	Life, Art, and Character of Shakespeare. 2 vols.	
	Cloth, retail	4.00
	New School Shakespeare. *Cloth.* Each Play .	.45
	Old School Shakespeare, per play	.20
	Expurgated Family Shakespeare	10.00
	Essays on Education, English Studies, etc. . .	.25
	Three Volume Shakespeare, per vol.	1.25
	Text-Book of Poetry	1.25
	Text-Book of Prose	1.25
	Pamphlet Selections, Prose and Poetry . . .	.15
	Classical English Reader	1.00
Johnson . .	Rasselas . . . . *Bds.,* .30; *Cloth,* .40	
Lee	Graphic Chart of English Literature	.25
Martineau .	The Peasant and the Prince . *Bds.,* .35; *Cloth,* .50	
Minto . . .	Manual of English Prose Literature	1.50
	Characteristics of English Poets	2.00
Rolfe	Craik's English of Shakespeare	.90
Scott	Guy Mannering . . . . . *Bds.,* .60; *Cloth,* .75	
	Ivanhoe . . . . *Bds.,* .60; *Cloth,* .75	
	Talisman . . . . *Bds.,* .50; *Cloth,* .60	
	Rob Roy . . . . *Bds.,* .60; *Cloth,* .75	
Sprague .	Milton's Paradise Lost, and Lycidas	.45
	Six Selections from Irving's Sketch-Book	
	Bds., .25; *Cloth,* .35	
Swift . . .	Gulliver's Travels . . . . *Bds.,* .30; *Cloth,* .40	
Thom	Shakespeare and Chaucer Examinations . . .	.00

GINN & COMPANY, Publishers,
Boston, New York, and Chicago.

www.ingramcontent.com/pod-product-compliance
Lightning Source LLC
Chambersburg PA
CBHW030615270326
41927CB00007B/1184